W9-CLX-789

COURSE 2

math INNOVATIONS

MOVING MATH FORWARD THROUGH CRITICAL THINKING AND EXPLORATION

Accent on Algebra

Focusing on Equations, Tables and Graphs

Suzanne H. Chapin

M. Katherine Gavin

Linda Jensen Sheffield

Kendall Hunt

p u b l i s h i n g   c o m p a n y

ACKNOWLEDGMENTS

Math Innovations Writing Team

Authors
Suzanne H. Chapin
M. Katherine Gavin
Linda Jensen Sheffield

Project Manager
Janice M. Vuolo

Teacher Edition Team
Jennifer M. MacPherson
Ann Marie Spinelli
Alice J. Gabbard

Writing Assistants
Jacob J. Whitmore
Kathy Dorkin
Jane Paulin

Mathematics Editor
Kathleen G. Snook

Assessment Specialist
Nancy Anderson

Advisory Board
Jerry P. Becker
Janet Beissinger
Diane J. Briars
Ann Lawrence
Ira J. Papick

Photo on pg. 30 is Public Domain. Images in book and on cover, unless otherwise noted, are used under license by ShutterStock, Inc.

Kendall Hunt
publishing company

www.kendallhunt.com
Send all inquiries to:
4050 Westmark Drive
Dubuque, IA 52004-1840
1-800-542-6657

Production Date: 10/8/12
Printed by: Hess Printing Solutions
Woodstock, Illinois
United States of America
Batch number: 42669604

Accent on Algebra:
Focusing on Equations, Tables and Graphs

Table of Contents

UNIT GOALS

Accent on Algebra: Focusing on Equations, Tables and Graphs

After studying this unit, you should be able to:

- Investigate and understand different uses of variables in expressions, equations, inequalities, formulas and properties with real numbers.

- Use the commutative, associative, identity, inverse, equality and distributive properties to simplify expressions and solve equations.

- Solve one-variable equations using a variety of methods.

- Represent linear relationships using tables, graphs, equations, words and diagrams.

- Write recursive and explicit rules for patterns identified in tables, graphs and drawings.

- Identify variable relationships as being either linear or nonlinear from tables, graphs and recursive rules.

Dear Student Mathematician,

Algebra is the language of mathematics. We use algebra to solve problems and express ideas in a generalized fashion. With algebra, we can express relationships between quantities using tables, graphs, pictures, words and symbols. Whether you are in business and use a spreadsheet to determine the cost of supplies from month to month or a jogger who wants to graph his or her speed when training, you can use algebra to represent ideas in ways that can be easily understood and applied again and again.

When working with numbers, we often notice patterns. We can represent these patterns using numbers, tables, graphs and words. But we can also represent patterns using symbols known as variables. In this unit, you will learn how variables are used in expressions, equations, inequalities, formulas and properties. You will learn how relationships between variables are expressed in tables, graphs and drawings. Finally, you will learn to classify relationships between variables as either linear or nonlinear.

An important part of algebra is solving equations and inequalities that involve variables. In Accent on Algebra, you will make sense of the steps used in solving equations and learn how number properties are at the heart of decision-making. You will use flowcharts and two solution methods, undoing and balancing, to solve equations. You also will perfect your skills for solving equations. Finally, you will graph inequalities on a number line to show solution sets.

We hope you enjoy the learning activities in this unit and that you gain a deeper understanding of algebraic representations.

Mathematically yours,
The Authors

Suzanne H. Chapin   *M. Katherine Gavin*   *Linda Sheffield*

SECTION 1

Understanding and Using Variables

Algebra is a powerful tool for understanding the world. You can represent ideas and relationships using symbols, tables and graphs. In this section you will learn about variables and investigate how they are used to model real situations. You may also learn some unusual facts about how people spend their free time!

LESSON 1.1 Variables

Start It Off

Marcelino was asked to find the area of a 43 in. by 8 in. rectangle using mental math. He drew this picture.

40 in.		3 in.
		8 in.

1. Marcelino found the areas of the two smaller rectangles and added them together. Why is this a useful application of the "mental math" method?

2. Which of these statements best represents his method? Why?

   A. $8 \cdot 43$
   $= 8(40 + 3)$
   $= 320 + 3$
   $= 323$

   B. $8 \cdot 43$
   $= 8(40 + 3)$
   $= 40 + 24$
   $= 64$

   C. $8 \cdot 43$
   $= 8(40 + 3)$
   $= 320 + 24$
   $= 344$

3. Marcelino's method is an example of the distributive property. Write down two things you know about the distributive property.

Are you interested in sports? Most students have a favorite sport they enjoy watching or playing. Mathematical symbols such as variables, operations and numbers can be used to represent and describe many situations associated with sports.

Algebraic Statements

Equations, expressions and inequalities are the building blocks of algebra. Examine the cards below.

A $4 \cdot 9 = 6 \cdot 6$

B $C = \pi d$

C $7m$

D $23 - x > 13$

E $y = -2x$

F $a + b = b + a$

G $36 + 8$

H $y = x - 1$

I $A = lw$

J $5 + 9 = n + 6$

K $14 - y$

L $a \cdot \frac{1}{a} = 1, a \neq 0$

M $35 = 7g$

N $5(3 + m) = 15 + 5m$

O $6 + s = 10$

P $4x - x = 3x$

Q $7x + 2y$

R $x < -4$

MATHEMATICALLY
SPEAKING

▶ equation
▶ inequality
▶ expression
▶ constant
▶ variable

1. a) Take a set of the cards and sort them into three groups—equations, inequalities and expressions.

b) How are the groups the same?

c) What do you think are the most important differences between expressions, equations and inequalities?

d) Write a definition for each of the terms: equation, expression and inequality.

2. a) Now sort the equation cards into different groups that you select.

b) Describe the cards in each group and explain why you put certain cards together.

c) Write two additional cards to add to each sorted group.

Many equations, inequalities and expressions have letters in them. Some letters are constants. A constant is a symbol that represents exactly one quantity. Every time the constant letter or symbol is used, the same value is substituted. The Greek letter π, called "pi," is an example of a constant. The value of π does not change; it is always the number equal to the circumference of a circle divided by the diameter of that circle.

Other letters, or symbols such as ❏ and Δ, are called variables. In equations, expressions and inequalities, one or more quantities can be substituted for a variable. In this lesson, you will learn about the different types of variables.

Variables Representing a Specific Value

Some variables represent a specific value. When you are asked to "solve an equation," you are to find the value of the variable that makes that equation true. This value is known as the solution. When variables represent specific values, there is often only one variable or letter in the equation.

> **Example 1**
>
> Major League Baseball teams play 162 games every season. In 2008, the San Diego Padres won 63 games. How many games did they lose?
>
> Let *n* represent the number of games the Padres lost.
>
> **Equation:** $63 + n = 162$
>
> **Solution:** $n = 99$ The Padres lost 99 games in the 2008 season.
>
> **Verify solution:** $63 + 99 = 162$

When asked to solve equations and find a specific value for a variable, we usually assume that the solution is a real number. But sometimes there are restrictions on which set of numbers can be used. This can affect the solutions.

Let's Review

Natural Numbers ($\mathbb{N}$)	$\{1, 2, 3, 4, 5, ...\}$
Whole Numbers	$\{0, 1, 2, 3, 4, 5, ...\}$
Integers ($\mathbb{Z}$)	$\{...-3, -2, -1, 0, 1, 2, 3, ...\}$
Rational Numbers ($\mathbb{Q}$)	Any number that can be expressed as $\frac{a}{b}$ where a and b are integers and $b \neq 0$
Real Numbers ($\mathbb{R}$)	Any number that can be represented on a number line

3. Find the solution to each equation below. Note which set of numbers can be used.

   a) $5x = {}^-15$ x belongs to the set of integers.

   b) $5x = {}^-15$ x belongs to the set of natural numbers.

   c) $2x = 13$ x belongs to the set of real numbers.

   d) $2x = 13$ x belongs to the set of integers.

Mathematicians use symbols to record information using the least number of words. Rather than write out the name of the set of numbers, they use its abbreviation. Another common abbreviation is the symbol, ϵ, which means "is an element of" or "is a member of."

$x \in \mathbb{Z}$ x is an element of the set of integers.

$x \in \mathbb{N}$ x is an element of the set of natural numbers.

$x \in \mathbb{R}$ x is an element of the set of real numbers.

4. Solve for n.

a) $\frac{2}{3}n = -\frac{1}{4}$ $n \in \mathbb{Z}$

b) $\frac{2}{3}n = 2$ $n \in \mathbb{N}$

c) $\frac{2}{3}n = -\frac{1}{4}$ $n \in \mathbb{R}$

5. Write an equation with a variable to represent each situation. Define the variable. Then, solve the equation. Be sure to check your answer by substituting the value back into the equation.

a) The total of two teams' scores for a basketball game was 176 points. One team scored 97 points. What was the other team's score?

b) How much time does it take a bicyclist to finish a 75-mile race if she averages 20 miles per hour?

c) Pole-vaulting is an athletic field event. Homer can pole-vault 2.5 times as high as Sally. If he can pole-vault 15 feet, how high can Sally pole-vault?

Variables Representing Related Varying Quantities

Some equations have two or more variables. If the value of one variable changes when the value of another variable changes, then there is a mathematical relationship that links the two variables. The variables represent related varying quantities. When two or more variables are mathematically related, there will be many different combinations of values for the variables that will make the equation true.

Example 2

Ticket prices for many baseball games depend on the opponent and the day of the week. If a ticket to the Chicago White Sox costs $15 for a specific Monday game, we can write an equation for finding the cost of any number of tickets to that game: $C = 15n$. In this case, n represents the number of tickets purchased and C represents their total cost in dollars.

Number of Tickets (n)	Cost in Dollars (C)
0	0
1	15
2	30
5	75
8	120

variable   variable

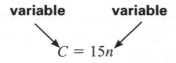

$$C = 15n$$

As the number of tickets, n, increases, the cost in dollars of the tickets, C, increases.

Since there are two variables in this equation, a solution must give a value for both n and C. These two values are often listed as an ordered pair, (n, C). The ordered pairs $(0, 0)$, $(1, 15)$, $(2, 30)$, $(5, 75)$ and $(8, 120)$ are some, but not all, of the solutions to this equation.

6. **a)** What do the variables n and C represent?

   b) Why are these variables referred to as "varying quantities"?

   c) What is the mathematical relationship between these quantities?

   d) List five other pairs of values that make the equation $C = 15n$ true. How many pairs of values are in the solution?

Variables Representing Many Values

You may have seen variables used in the statement of mathematical properties. For example, the commutative property of addition states that $a + b = b + a$, for all real numbers a and b. It is important to realize that a and b are not mathematically related. In other words, changing the value of a does not change the value of b. Rather, a and b are being used as "generalized numbers." The statement $a + b = b + a$ is true for any real numbers a and b.

Variables in mathematical properties generalize important ideas. The variables can represent many values and are not related. Examine the equations below. These equations are true for all values of the variable(s). The variables can equal any real numbers. Not all of these statements are properties.

$$a + a = 2a \qquad\qquad a + b - b = a$$

$$a + b = b + a \qquad\qquad a \cdot (b \cdot c) = (a \cdot b) \cdot c$$

7. Write three different equations that use variables as "generalized numbers." Are each of the equations you wrote a property?

An inequality is one type of mathematical sentence that expresses a relationship between numbers and variables. Variables in inequalities usually represent a set of values. This in turn means that there usually are many solutions to an inequality.

Example 3

At one time Major League Soccer players had a cap on their salaries of $2 million. This restriction can be written using the inequality $x \le 2{,}000{,}000$, where x is the salary in whole numbers of dollars.

$$x \le 2{,}000{,}000 \qquad\qquad\qquad x \in \text{whole numbers}$$

The solution for x is the set of whole numbers between 0 and 2,000,000, including 0 and 2,000,000. That is, salaries can be from $0 through $2 million.

A variable in an inequality often represents many values. The solution to an inequality can be graphed on a number line. When a solid point is used on a graph, it means that the point is a solution. When an open point or circle is used, it means that the point does not satisfy the stated relationship and is not a solution. A ray on the number line includes all possible points along the ray. In the following examples, $x \in \mathbb{R}$.

$$x \le 2\tfrac{1}{2} \qquad\qquad\qquad x < 2\tfrac{1}{2}$$

$2\tfrac{1}{2}$ is in the set of values that make this statement true.

$2\tfrac{1}{2}$ is not in the set of values that make this statement true.

Number line graphs look different depending on the set of numbers used.

Example 4

How does the set of numbers used for the variable affect the graph of the inequality?

If the variable is a member of the integers, then the set of values that makes the inequality true will be integers. Thus, only integers are marked on the number line.

Graph $x > {}^-3$ $x \in \mathbb{Z}$

$$\longleftarrow\!\!+\!\!+\!\!+\!\!+\!\!+\!\!+\!\!+\!\!+\!\!+\!\!\bullet\!\!\bullet\!\!\bullet\!\!\bullet\!\!\bullet\!\!\bullet\!\!\bullet\!\!\bullet\!\!\bullet\!\!\bullet\!\!\bullet\!\!\bullet\!\!\bullet\!\!\longrightarrow$$
$$^-10\ ^-9\ ^-8\ ^-7\ ^-6\ ^-5\ ^-4\ ^-3\ ^-2\ ^-1\ 0\ 1\ 2\ 3\ 4\ 5\ 6\ 7\ 8\ 9\ 10$$

If the variable is a member of the real numbers, then the set of values that makes the inequality true will be real numbers. A solid arrow is used to show that all fraction and decimal values make the inequality true.

Graph $x > {}^-3$ $x \in \mathbb{R}$

$$\longleftarrow\!\!+\!\!+\!\!+\!\!+\!\!+\!\!+\!\!+\!\!\circ\!\!-\!\!-\!\!-\!\!-\!\!-\!\!-\!\!-\!\!-\!\!-\!\!-\!\!-\!\!-\!\!\longrightarrow$$
$$^-10\ ^-9\ ^-8\ ^-7\ ^-6\ ^-5\ ^-4\ ^-3\ ^-2\ ^-1\ 0\ 1\ 2\ 3\ 4\ 5\ 6\ 7\ 8\ 9\ 10$$

8. List some numbers that satisfy the following conditions. Then graph the solution to these inequalities on a number line. Note the sets of numbers used.

a) $x \geq 1$ $x \in \mathbb{R}$

b) $x < {}^-4$ $x \in \mathbb{Z}$

c) $23 - x > 13$ $x \in \mathbb{Z}$

d) How would the graph of Part b change if x were a real number? A whole number?

Think Beyond

e) $x < {}^-4$ or $x \geq 1$ $x \in \mathbb{Z}$

Variables in Expressions

MATHEMATICALLY SPEAKING

▶ evaluate

Unlike an equation, an expression cannot be true or false. So, you cannot "solve" an expression. However, if you are given specific values for the variables, you can "evaluate" the expression. This means you substitute the values of the variables into the expression and simplify.

Example 5

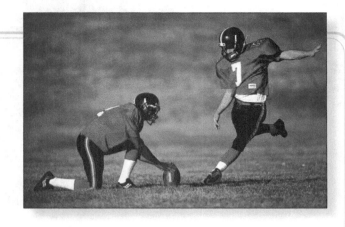

In football, a team gets 3 points for every field goal. You can represent the points obtained by field goals with the expression $3m$, where m stands for the number of field goals. You can evaluate this expression for specific values of the variable.

To find the number of points scored in four field goals, substitute 4 for m.

$$3m = 3(4) = 12$$

The value of an expression can change. If there are five field goals, you substitute 5 for m. The expression now is equivalent to $3 \cdot 5$, and its value is 15.

9. Examine the set of cards from earlier in the lesson. Sort the cards with variables into the following groups:

   Group 1: The variables each represent one specific value.

   Group 2: The variables represent related varying quantities.

   Group 3: The variables represent many values.

   Group 4: Cards that don't fit into Groups 1–3

10. Use cards C, K and Q from the set you used earlier in the lesson. Evaluate these cards when $m = {}^-4$, $y = {}^-1$, and $x = \frac{1}{2}$.

**rap It Up**

Variables can be used in different ways. Explain these uses and how variables can be used in algebra.

Write About It

1. Explain the three ways that variables are used in equations and inequalities.

2. Is it possible to "solve" an expression? Why or why not?

3. Kayla sorted the algebra cards in the following way. Describe her sorting plan.

Group 1

$7x + 2y$
$a + b = b + a$
$y = {}^-2x$
$y = x - 1$

Group 2

$A = lw$
$C = \pi d$

Group 3

$36 + 8$
$4 \cdot 9 = 6 \cdot 6$

Group 4

$5(3 + m) = 15 + 5m$
$23 - x > 13$
$7m$
$a \cdot \frac{1}{a} = 1, a \neq 0$
$6 + s = 10$
$35 = 7g$
$5 + 9 = n + 6$
$4x - x = 3x$
$14 - y$
$x < {}^-4$

4. Evaluate the following expressions first for $y = {}^-6$ and then for $y = \frac{1}{3}$.

   a) $14 - y$ b) $7y$ c) $3y + 2y$ d) $6\left(y + \frac{1}{2}\right)$

5. You may have classified some of the equations in the card activity as properties and others as formulas. Give your own example of a property and of a formula.

6. Create an example for each of the situations below. State the set of numbers you are using.

   a) an equation with variables that represent related varying quantities

   b) a property with one or more variables that represent many values

   c) an equation with one or more variables that represent specific values

   d) an inequality with a variable that represents a set of numbers

7. A new student in your class has never learned about variables. Tell him what he needs to know about variables in order for him to make sense of their use in equations and expressions. Identify the values the variables can assume.

8. Match the phrases to the mathematical expressions.

   a) 2 more than x i) $\frac{1}{2}x$

   b) 2 times the value of x ii) $5 + 2x$

   c) the value of x reduced by 2   iii) $x + 2$

   d) 2 times the value of x plus 5   iv) $x - 2$

   e) half of x v) $2x$

9. Graph each inequality on a number line.

   Hint
   See page 157

   a) $-3 < x$ $x \in \mathbb{Z}$

   b) $x \le 2$ $x \in \mathbb{Z}$

   c) $4.5 > x$ $x \in \mathbb{R}$

   d) $x \ge -\frac{1}{2}$ $x \in \mathbb{R}$

10. Calvin raised $150 for charity. He plans to divide it equally between n charities so that each group receives D dollars.

    a) Write an equation that shows how Calvin plans to distribute the money.

    b) How are the variables used in this equation?

    c) Describe values for n that make sense in this situation.

11. In a basketball game, a basket made on a free throw is worth 1 point, baskets made from inside the 3-point line are worth 2 points, and those made from outside the 3-point line are worth 3 points. Use variables to write an equation for the total score of one team for each game. Explain what each of your variables represents.

12. How are the ages of your family members related to you? Let x represent your age today in years.

   a) Write two different expressions using x that represent the ages of two people in your family.

   ? Hint
   See page 157

   b) Evaluate each expression for $x = 5$. What does the value of each expression mean?

13. Write the following expressions using variables.

   a) 7 less than n

   b) 9 times y

   c) the sum of x and 5, divided by 2

   d) 12 more than s

   e) the product of 5 and w decreased by $^-4$

   f) k times the sum of a and b

14. There are many types of mathematical statements in algebra. How are they similar and how are they different? Give examples.

Think
Beyond

15. In mathematics, the Greek letter π represents a constant. Are there other letters or symbols mathematicians use to represent constants? Investigate this question using the Internet and write a report for the class.

16. What is the height of this parallelogram?

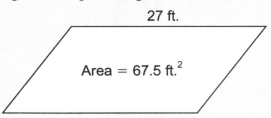

27 ft.

Area = 67.5 ft.^{2}

   A. 2.5 ft.   **C.** 1,822.5 ft.

   B. 2.5 ft.^{2} **D.** 1,822.5 ft.^{2}

17. Evaluate: $17 + (^-28) \div (^-2) - 45$.

18. Solve: $\frac{2}{3}s = 14$. Show your work.

19. Is the following equation always, sometimes or never true? $\triangle$ and $\bigcirc$ represent real numbers. Explain your answer.

$$\triangle \bullet \bigcirc = {}^-\triangle \bullet {}^-\bigcirc$$

20. If a recipe uses 114 chocolate chips to make 12 giant cookies, what is the average number of chocolate chips per giant cookie?

➡️ **Start It Off**

Sam drew the following rectangle to help him compute the product of 37 and 15 mentally.

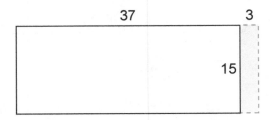

1. Why do you think Sam made the rectangle larger instead of dividing it into two smaller rectangles?

2. Here is what Sam wrote. Discuss what it means with your partner. Why is he multiplying 15 by 40 and then subtracting 45?

$$15 \cdot 37 = 15 \cdot 40 - 15 \cdot 3$$
$$= 600 - 45$$
$$= 555$$

3. Use Sam's method and this rectangle to help you find the product of 5 and 29. What numbers will you multiply and what number will you subtract?

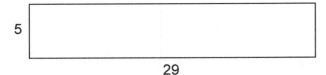

4. Calculate $99 \cdot 7$ mentally using this method.

Using Formulas

A formula is an equation that is used to solve specific types of problems. For example, elite athletes, like the runner Veronica Campbell, use formulas to determine their heart rate during different types of training exercises. One formula enables athletes to determine their maximum heart rate. This is the greatest number of beats per minute that a heart should beat during exercise.

$$H = 206.9 - 0.67x$$

In this formula, H represents maximum heart rate in beats per minute and x represents age in years.

Example

What is the maximum heart rate for a 30-year-old?

To use this formula to find the maximum heart rate for a 30-year-old, substitute 30 for the age variable, x, and evaluate the expression on the right side of the equation to find the corresponding maximum heart rate, H.

$$H = 206.9 - 0.67x$$
$$= 206.9 - (0.67 \cdot 30)$$
$$= 206.9 - 20.1$$
$$= 186.8 \text{ beats/min.}$$

The maximum heart rate for a 30-year-old is about 187 beats per minute.

1. **a)** Use the maximum heart rate formula to find your maximum heart rate.

   b) What is the maximum heart rate of someone who is 40 years old? 50 years old? 60 years old?

Many of the formulas you have learned so far are generalized rules that involve measures such as area, volume, circumference, distance, angle sums and perimeter. For example, $A = lw$ is the formula for finding the area of *any* rectangle. What other formulas do you know?

Formula Match-Up

Review common measurement formulas by playing the game
Formula Match-Up.

 · · · · · · · · · **Formula Match-Up** · · · · · · · · ·

Players: 2–3 people

Materials: Formula Match-Up game cards

DIRECTIONS:

1. The goal is to match cards that represent the same formula. Some cards display a formula using symbols, some cards explain a formula in words and some cards have a word problem that you can solve using a specific formula.

2. Shuffle the cards and arrange them in a 6-by-6 array, face down.

3. A player turns over three cards. If all three cards match (formula, words, word problem), the player keeps them. Players check each other's matches to make sure they all represent the same formula. If all three cards do not match, the player turns the cards over and leaves them on the table.

4. Players take turns turning cards over to find matches.

5. The game is over when all cards have been chosen or no more matches are possible. The player with the most cards is the winner.

2. Play Formula Match-Up.

3. Choose three of the formula cards. For each formula, write a new word problem that can be solved using the formula. Work with a partner.

4. Trade the word problems you wrote with another pair of students. Match these new problems to the formulas in the Formula Match-Up set.

5. Separate all the word problems from the deck of cards. Take turns selecting a word problem and stating which formula you would use to solve the problem on the card. Also describe what each variable in the formula represents.

 **rap It Up**

Formulas are handy rules for solving problems. Discuss how you might group the different types of formulas on the Formula Match-Up cards. Explain how you remember different formulas.

MATHEMATICALLY SPEAKING

▶ formula

Write
About It

1. Carla stated, "If the area of a rectangle is 20 square centimeters, and I can use any type of number for length and width, then there are an infinite number of possibilities for the length and the width. But if the area is 20 square centimeters and the length of this rectangle is 5 cm, then there is only one possible value for the width. The meaning of the variables in the formula, $A = lw$, confuses me. Do the variables stand for many values or for specific numbers, and do they vary in relationship to each other? Can the meaning be different depending on the situation?" Respond to Carla.

2. What strategies do you use to help you remember and use certain formulas correctly?

Use the following information and formula to answer Questions 3–5.

A person's surface area is the amount of skin that covers his or her body. Healthcare workers sometimes use estimates of the surface area of a patient's body to decide how much medication he or she should receive. One way to approximate a person's surface area is to use the following formula:

height (cm) • thigh circumference (cm) • 2 = body surface area (cm²)

3. a) Rewrite the formula for body surface area using letters and numbers. Define what each of the letters represents in this formula.

   b) Many formulas are written in terms of metric measurements. Why do you think this is the case?

4. a) Use the formula to find the surface area of a child who is 102 cm tall and has a thigh circumference of 40 cm.

Think
Beyond

   b) Find the surface area in square inches of a person who is 5 feet tall and has a thigh circumference of 19 inches.

5. If a person has a thigh circumference of 54 cm and a body surface area of about 19,440 cm², what is his or her approximate height in centimeters?

6. The formula $F = \frac{9}{5}C + 32$ is used to convert temperatures from degrees Celsius to degrees Fahrenheit. The variable F represents the temperature in degrees Fahrenheit, and the variable C represents the temperature in degrees Celsius. Use the formula to convert the following temperatures into degrees Fahrenheit. Show your work.

   a) 0°C

   b) 6°C

   c) 20°C

   d) 32°C

   e) −15°C

7. Find the areas of the following polygons.

   Hint
   See page 157

   a)

   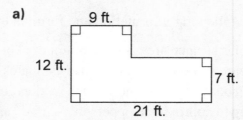

   b)

   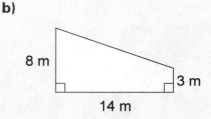

8. Maple syrup comes from the sap of maple trees. Big trees produce more sap—a minimum tree diameter of 12 inches is recommended. You can measure the diameter of a tree with a special tool, called calipers.

   a) If you have only a tape measure, what dimension(s) can you measure on a tree?

   b) If you know the circumference of a tree, what formula can you use to figure out the diameter?

   c) Patricia has been asked to identify the maple trees on the school property that can be used for syrup. She can only mark trees that have a diameter of at least 12 inches. She has only a tape measure. Give Patricia suggestions for how she can do this.

9. a) What is the sum of the measures of the interior angles on a YIELD sign?

Hint
See page 157

Think Beyond

b) Think about the shape of traffic signs. Determine the sum of the interior angles on four different signs such as STOP signs or speed limit signs.

Hint
See page 157

10. Beatrice sorted the following equations into two categories: formulas and not formulas. Explain why you agree or disagree with her classification. If necessary, place the equations in the correct category.

Formulas	**Not Formulas**
$D = rt$	$d = 2r$
$b \div 1 = b$	$a + {}^-a = 0$
$A = \pi r^2$	$P = 2l + 2w$
$(a \cdot b) \cdot c = a \cdot (b \cdot c)$	$A = bh$

11. Archaeologists use formulas to estimate the height of a person based on the length of his or her tibia, or shinbone. The variable h represents a person's height, and the variable t represents the length of a tibia. Both measurements are in centimeters.

females: $h = 72.572 + 2.533t$

males: $h = 81.688 + 2.392t$

a) What is the approximate height of a female if the length of her tibia is 36 centimeters?

b) What is the approximate height of a male in centimeters if the length of his tibia is 40 centimeters?

Tibia

Think Beyond

c) Determine your own height in centimeters. Use your height to approximate the length of your tibia. Remember 1 inch is approximately equal to 2.54 centimeters.

12. Use the formula $H = 206.9 - 0.67x$ to calculate the maximum heart rate of a healthy person who is:

a) 43 years old   **b)** 75 years old   **c)** 11 years old

Think Beyond

13. Formulas are commonly used in science. Create a Science Formula Match-Up game. Play the game with your classmates.

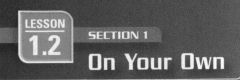

14. Find the formula for converting degrees Fahrenheit to degrees Celsius and then determine the temperatures in degrees Celsius for each of the following.

a) −18°F   b) 95°F   c) 70°F   d) 55°F   e) 21°F

f) Compare the Fahrenheit-to-Celsius formula to the Celsius-to-Fahrenheit formula. How are these formulas related?

15. Mrs. Ryer's land is shaped like a trapezoid. Find the area and perimeter of Mrs. Ryer's land.

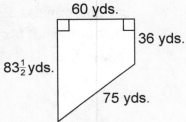

60 yds.

36 yds.

$83\frac{1}{2}$ yds.

75 yds.

16. Show how this expression can be simplified using factors: $-\frac{7}{15} \cdot \frac{3}{56}$

17. Find a rule for a sequence whose first four terms are 12, 9, 6 and 3, and then use that rule to determine the 5th, 6th and 7th terms of the sequence.

18. Find the missing angle measures without using a protractor.

a) parallelogram $ABCD$

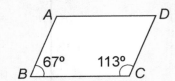

67°   113°

b) triangle CAT

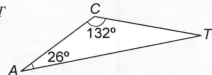

132°   26°

19. It costs $0.10 to make a cup of lemonade. Alex and Carla are selling cups of lemonade for $0.25 each. How much profit will they make if they make and sell 40 cups of lemonade?

A. $4.00   D. $6.00

B. $10.00   E. none of these

C. $14.00

Mathematical Properties

➡️ **Start It Off**

Indicate whether A is true, B is true, both A and B are true or neither A nor B is true.

	A	**B**
1.	$6^2 \cdot 2^1 = 24$	$6^1 \cdot 2^2 = 72$
2.	$\frac{3}{7} \cdot \frac{4}{7} = \frac{12}{49}$	$\frac{4}{7} \cdot \frac{3}{7} = \frac{12}{7^2}$
3.	$15 = 2 \cdot 4 + 7$	$22 = 2 \cdot 4 + 7$
4.	$5(6 + 11) = 5(6) + 11$	$5(6 + 11) = 11(6) + 5(11)$
5.	$\frac{3}{4} \cdot \frac{2}{9} = \frac{2}{4} \cdot \frac{3}{9}$	$\frac{5}{8} \cdot \frac{2}{10} = \frac{2}{8} \cdot \frac{5}{10}$

6. In the equations in Question 5, the numerators are switched. Simplify the fractions with switched numerators. What do you notice? Why might you want to switch the numerators in these multiplication problems?

In mathematics, the way we order and group numbers is very important. Depending on the operations involved, you can sometimes change the order and grouping of numbers and variables, but sometimes you cannot. Mathematical properties describe these important relationships.

Mathematical properties also help us to perform and simplify calculations. You will need to know and understand these properties in order to manipulate symbols accurately and efficiently.

Ordering Properties

MATHEMATICALLY SPEAKING

▶ commutative property of addition

▶ commutative property of multiplication

Certain properties involve the order of the numbers and variables in an expression or equation. The order of two numbers or variables in an addition or multiplication problem does not change the resulting sum or product. In other words, two real numbers can be added or multiplied in either order, and the result is the same. These properties are known as the commutative properties:

• **commutative property of addition**: For any real numbers a and b, $a + b = b + a$.

• **commutative property of multiplication**: For any real numbers a and b, $a \cdot b = b \cdot a$.

To commute means to change the order of two things. Lots of times the order you do things in doesn't matter. But other times the order in which you perform actions, such as "taking a shower" and "taking your clothes off," makes a difference—these actions are not commutative.

1. Think of a pair of everyday actions where the order in which they are performed does not matter (they are commutative) and a pair where the order in which they are performed does make a difference (they are not commutative).

2. **a)** Write an equation that illustrates the commutative property of addition and an equation that illustrates the commutative property of multiplication.

   b) Why do the definitions of properties include conditions, such as "for any real numbers a and b"?

Identity Elements and Inverses Using Addition and Subtraction

Does order matter when subtracting? That is, is subtraction commutative?

3. **a)** Copy and fill in the table. In the last two rows, choose your own values for a and b.

a	b	$a - b = ?$	$b - a = ?$	Differences
9	3	$9 - 3 = 6$	$3 - 9 = ^-6$	6 and $^-6$
1	$^-7$			
6.5	3.4			
$^-5$	$^-9$			
12	12			
$\frac{5}{6}$	$\frac{1}{6}$			
5	2			

   b) Describe any patterns in the pairs of differences. What do we call these pairs of numbers?

   c) Is the operation of subtraction commutative? Explain.

4. a) What number added to each of the numbers 2.7, -36 and $-\frac{2}{5}$ gives a sum of 0? Recall that a number and its opposite are called additive inverses. The sum of additive inverses is zero.

b) What is the additive inverse of 0? of a? of $-a$?

c) Why is zero such an important number when adding?

• **additive inverse** property: For every real number a, $a + (-a) = 0$.

• **identity property of addition**: For every real number a, $a + 0 = a$ and
$$0 + a = a.$$

The identity, or "identity element," for addition is 0. Put another way, 0 is the additive identity of the real numbers—adding zero does not change the value of a real number.

5. a) Jaime uses additive inverses and identities when she calculates mentally. She changes $37 + 98$ to $35 + 100$. This can be shown mathematically as
$(37 + (-2)) + (98 + 2) = 35 + 100$.
Explain how Jaime used additive inverses and the identity property of addition to make a simpler, but equivalent, calculation.

b) Rewrite the following expressions as "easier" sums for calculating mentally. Use additive inverses and the identity property to show why your rewrites are equivalent to the original expressions.

i) $357 + 73$ **iii)** $999 + 658$

ii) $4,015 + 596$ **iv)** $9\frac{19}{20} + 1\frac{4}{5}$

Identity Elements and Inverses Using Multiplication and Division

Is division commutative? Let's investigate what happens when you change the order of the numbers in division expressions.

6. a) Copy and complete the table. For the last two rows, choose your own values for *a* and *b*. Keep all answers in fraction form.

a	b	a ÷ b = ?	b ÷ a = ?	Quotients
−10	2	−10 ÷ 2 = −5	2 ÷ −10 = $-\frac{1}{5}$	−5 and $-\frac{1}{5}$
36	9			
$\frac{1}{2}$	3			
−10	−4			
$\frac{2}{3}$	$\frac{3}{2}$			
$\frac{7}{5}$	$-\frac{1}{10}$			

b) Compare the quotient of the first division problem to the quotient of the division problem created by switching the two numbers. Describe patterns you notice among these pairs of quotients.

c) Is division commutative?

Recall that reciprocals are two numbers whose product is 1. You use reciprocals when dividing fractions. We also call a number and its reciprocal, such as -4 and $-\frac{1}{4}$, multiplicative inverses.

• **multiplicative inverse** property: For every real number *a* where $a \neq 0$,
$$a \cdot \frac{1}{a} = 1.$$

The number 1 is the "identity element" for multiplication. That is, multiplying any number by 1 does not change the value of the original number. This is stated formally as the identity property of multiplication.

• **identity property of multiplication**: For every real number *a*, $a \cdot 1 = a$ and $1 \cdot a = a$.

A costume can change your appearance without changing your identity. A similar situation occurs all the time in mathematics. The identity or value of a number is left unchanged when you apply the identity property of multiplication and multiply by 1. But the number may appear different. For example, $\frac{1}{2}$ and $\frac{3}{6}$ represent the same number. Multiplying $\frac{1}{2}$ by 1 in the form of $\frac{3}{3}$ gives $\frac{3}{6}$.
$$\frac{1}{2} \cdot \frac{3}{3} = \frac{3}{6}$$

7. a) Give the multiplicative inverse of $-7, \frac{2}{5}, -3\frac{3}{8}, \frac{1}{9}$ and -16.

b) Write three statements using the terms *multiplicative inverses, reciprocals* and *identity element* to describe the relationship between the numbers in the Quotients column in the table for Question 6.

c) What is the multiplicative inverse of 0?

Mental math techniques for multiplication also are useful to know. The following techniques work because of the identity property and multiplicative inverses.

Strategy 1

halve and double: Double one factor and halve the other factor to make multiplication easier. You can do this repeatedly.

$8 \cdot 4 = 16 \cdot 2 = 32 \cdot 1 = 32$

Strategy 2

multiply then divide: Multiply one of the factors by a number, n, to form a power of 10. Multiply the factors by the reciprocal of n.

$25 \cdot 12 = [(25 \cdot 4) \cdot 12] \cdot \frac{1}{4} = 1{,}200 \cdot \frac{1}{4} = 300$

8. Copy the following

Strategy 1

$$18 \cdot 16 = (18 \cdot 2) \cdot \left(16 \cdot \frac{1}{2}\right)$$
$$= 36 \cdot 8$$
$$= (36 \cdot 2) \cdot \left(8 \cdot \frac{1}{2}\right)$$
$$= 72 \cdot 4$$
$$= (72 \cdot 2) \cdot \left(4 \cdot \frac{1}{2}\right)$$
$$= 144 \cdot 2$$
$$= 288$$

Strategy 2

$$27 \cdot 5 = [27 \cdot (5 \cdot 2)] \cdot \frac{1}{2}$$
$$= 270 \cdot \frac{1}{2}$$
$$= 135$$

a) Underline the multiplicative inverses. Why doesn't multiplying by inverses change the products?

b) How was the identity property of multiplication used to form equivalent expressions?

Grouping Properties

Look at the following expressions. Which two numbers would you add or multiply first to make mental calculations easier?

$$38 \cdot 4 \cdot 25 \qquad 189 + 37 + 13 \qquad \frac{3}{2} \cdot 0.\overline{6} \cdot {}^{-}36$$

The associative properties of addition and multiplication of real numbers state that how numbers and variables are grouped in an addition expression or in a multiplication expression does not affect the sums or products. So, in the expressions above, rather than perform the computations in order from left to right, you can group the addends or factors to make the computation as easy as possible; the results will be the same.

$$38 \cdot (4 \cdot 25) \qquad 189 + (37 + 13) \qquad \left(\frac{3}{2} \cdot 0.\overline{6}\right) \cdot {}^{-}36$$

The associative properties are usually stated using variables.

• associative property of addition: For all real numbers a, b, c,
$$a + (b + c) = (a + b) + c.$$

• associative property of multiplication: For all real numbers a, b, c,
$$a \cdot (b \cdot c) = (a \cdot b) \cdot c.$$

9. **a)** Is the operation of subtraction associative? In other words, does it matter how you group the numbers in a subtraction expression? Use the example, $(15 - 10) - 1$ and $15 - (10 - 1)$.

   b) Is the operation of division associative? In other words, does it matter how you group the numbers in a division expression? Use the example, $16 \div (8 \div 2)$ and $(16 \div 8) \div 2$.

   c) Consider the rules for the order of operations. Why do you think the rules state "perform multiplication and division in the order given from left to right" and "perform addition and subtraction in the order given from left to right"?

10. Rewrite each expression using parentheses to show which operation should be performed first to simplify the calculation. You may need to change the order of the numbers. Find the value of each expression.

   a) $-\frac{5}{8} + 1\frac{2}{3} + \frac{3}{8} + \frac{2}{8}$

   b) $\frac{3}{4} + 9.7 + {}^-0.75$

   c) $\frac{1}{7} \cdot 2\frac{2}{5} \cdot \frac{5}{12}$

   d) $\frac{5}{12} \cdot 0.\overline{3} \cdot 3$

 **Wrap It Up**

What are inverses? Why are they important? How can inverses and identity properties be used with the commutative and associative properties to create "easier" equivalent expressions?

MATHEMATICALLY
SPEAKING

▶ additive inverse

▶ associative property of addition

▶ associative property of multiplication

▶ commutative property of addition

▶ commutative property of multiplication

▶ identity element

▶ identity property of addition

▶ identity property of multiplication

▶ multiplicative inverse

 **Write About It**

1. Make a small poster about the commutative, associative and identity properties. Be sure to include examples of how these properties can be used to simplify calculations.

2. The following expressions are missing a value. For each, pick two different values that if inserted would result in "easy" calculations because of identity and inverse properties. Evaluate the expressions.

   a) $68 + \underline{\hspace{1cm}} + 17$ **c)** $^{-}82 + \underline{\hspace{1cm}} + 246$

   b) $4 \cdot \underline{\hspace{1cm}} \cdot \frac{5}{6}$ **d)** $\underline{\hspace{1cm}} (^{-}25)(92)$

3. Decide whether the following pairs of activities are commutative. Explain your reasoning.

   a) "brush your teeth" and "eat breakfast"

   b) "score the only point" and "win the game"

   c) "do your homework" and "watch TV"

4. Match each item in Column I with the correct choice(s) from Column II. Choices may be used once, more than once or not at all.

I		II	
a)	additive inverse of a	**i)**	1
b)	an example of multiplicative inverses	**ii)**	0
c)	the only number that has no multiplicative inverse	**iii)**	$(7 \cdot 2) \cdot 5 = 7 \cdot (2 \cdot 5)$
d)	an example of a commutative property	**iv)**	equation
e)	an example of an associative property	**v)**	$\frac{3}{5}$ and $1\frac{2}{3}$
f)	multiplicative inverse of the nonzero number a	**vi)**	$65 + 79 = 64 + 80$
g)	a statement that two expressions are equal	**vii)**	expression
h)	the number that is its own additive inverse	**viii)**	$\frac{1}{a}$
i)	the two numbers that are their own multiplicative inverses	**ix)**	^{-}a
j)	a collection of numbers, variables, operation symbols and/or grouping symbols	**x)**	$^{-}1$
		xi)	$7 \cdot y = y \cdot 7$

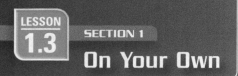
5. Write one addition and one multiplication expression using three or more fractions and/or decimals where the calculations can be simplified when you change the order and/or grouping of the terms. Rewrite the expressions and then evaluate them.

6. How is the variable in a property different from the variable in an equation such as $m - 8 = 17$?

7. What was Jane's mistake when she simplified the following expression: $8 - (^-8) = 0$?

8. Make a list of the mathematical properties you know. State each property using variables and then give an example using numbers.

Hint
See page 157

Think Beyond

9. Allison's little sister is learning to divide fractions. She says to Allison, "It is so easy! All you have to do is flip over the divisor and then multiply." Allison asked her sister why that works, but her sister couldn't explain. How could Allison help her sister understand why she can divide fractions by multiplying by the reciprocal?

Hint
See page 157

10. You use the identity property of multiplication to multiply a fraction by 1 to form an equivalent fraction. You can also divide by 1, the identity element, to simplify an expression. Simplify each expression below. Show how the two expressions are equivalent using the identity property of multiplication $\left(\text{for example, } \frac{32}{24} \div 1 = \frac{32}{24} \div \frac{8}{8} = \frac{4}{3} \right)$.

a) $-\frac{13}{39}$

c) $\frac{72}{64x}$

b) $\frac{49}{35}$

d) $\frac{24y}{36}$

11. For expressions i–iv below:

   a) Rewrite the expression with parentheses to make mental calculation easier.

   b) Evaluate the expression.

   c) State all properties you used. For example, if you changed the order of two factors or addends, you applied the commutative property of multiplication or addition.

   i) $1.36 + 0.7 + 0.64 + 3.17$

   ii) $2.\overline{6} + 5.018 + \frac{1}{3}$

   iii) $\frac{6}{10} \cdot \frac{3}{5} \cdot \frac{10}{6}$

   iv) $\frac{4}{5} \cdot 0.5 \cdot 1.2$

Think Back

12. Tanner's grandfather explained that it takes him an average of 13 minutes to play one hole of golf.

   a) Write an expression with a variable for this situation. State what the variable represents.

   b) Using this expression, how long will it take Tanner's grandfather to play 18 holes of golf? Write your answer in "hours : minutes" format.

13. Dani is measuring the length of a butterfly's wings for a science project. What metric measurement unit should she use and why?

14. Identify the solution to this equation: $125 = \frac{x}{50}$.

   A. 75   B. 6,250   C. 2.5   D. 175

15. Find a recursive rule for a sequence whose first four terms are 0.0278, 0.278, 2.78 and 27.8.
   Use this rule to determine the 5th, 6th and 7th terms of the sequence.

16. The distance formula states that the distance you travel is equal to the product of your speed and the time you spend traveling. In other words, $D = rt$ where D is the distance, r is the rate or speed and t is the time traveled.

   Alessandro rode his bike at an average speed of $6\frac{1}{2}$ miles per hour for a total of $5\frac{1}{4}$ hours. What distance did Alessandro travel?

   Answer the question and show your work. Write your answer as a mixed number and as an improper fraction. Be sure to label your answer.

The Distributive Property

➡️ Start It Off

Use mental math to find the missing value that creates a true statement.

1. ☐ · 5 = 16 · 10

2. 64 + 57 = ☐ + 60

3. 7.04 − 1.98 = 7.06 − ☐

4. 78 · ☐ = 39 · 32

5. Explain, in writing, how you found your answers to Questions 2 and 4.

Ultimate is a noncontact team sport played with a flying disc, usually referred to as a Frisbee®. As in football, players score points by passing the disc into the end zone. However, players cannot move when holding the disc.

1. Ultimate is played on a large field. Determine the area of the field in two different ways.

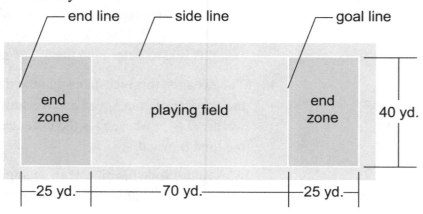

MATHEMATICALLY SPEAKING

- distributive property of multiplication over addition
- distributive property of multiplication over subtraction

The distributive property of multiplication over addition of real numbers enables you to turn the product of a factor and a sum into a sum of smaller, more manageable products. Did you multiply 40 (the width of the field) by each of the shorter lengths and then add the areas together? Or did you first add all the lengths together and then multiply by 40? Method 1 below uses the distributive property of multiplication over addition.

Method 1: $40(25 + 70 + 25) = 40(25) + 40(70) + 40(25)$

$= 1{,}000 + 2{,}800 + 1{,}000$

$= 4{,}800$

The area of the field is 4,800 yd.^2

Method 2: $40(25 + 70 + 25) = 40(120)$

$= 4{,}800$

The area of the field is 4,800 yd.^2

2. Compare both solution methods. What do you think it means to "distribute" multiplication over addition?

You can also use the distributive property of multiplication over subtraction. For example, when multiplying 56 • 99, it is easier to think of the 99 as 100 − 1.

Example

Find 56 • 99.

First rewrite 99 as 100 − 1. You can then distribute the multiplication by 56 to both values.

$$\begin{aligned} 56 \cdot 99 &= 56(100 - 1) \\ &= (56 \cdot 100) - (56 \cdot 1) \\ &= 5{,}600 - 56 \\ &= 5{,}544 \end{aligned}$$

The diagram below represents 56(100 − 1).
The shaded portion represents the area to be subtracted.

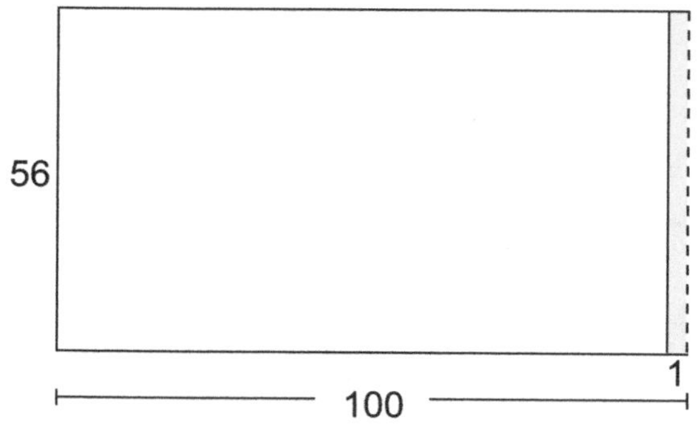

The distributive properties are usually stated formally using variables.

- distributive property of multiplication over addition:
  For each real number, a, b, and c,
  $$a(b + c) = ab + ac \quad \text{and} \quad ab + ac = a(b + c).$$

- distributive property of multiplication over subtraction:
  For each real number, a, b, and c,
  $$a(b - c) = ab - ac \quad \text{and} \quad ab - ac = a(b - c).$$

The distributive property is often used when computing mentally. Break up the multiplication into parts, calculate each part separately, and then add or subtract the results.

$$7 \cdot 38 \qquad\qquad \text{Think: } 7 \cdot (40 - 2)$$

Distribute the "$7 \cdot$" to both 40 and 2:
$$7(40 - 2) = 7(40) - 7(2)$$
$$= 280 - 14$$
$$= 266$$

3. Use the distributive property to find these products using mental math. Show mathematically how you distributed the multiplication.

   a) $5 \cdot 87$

   b) $124 \cdot 3$

   c) $\$1.98 \cdot 4$

   d) $49 \cdot 16$

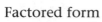

MATHEMATICALLY SPEAKING

▶ factored form

▶ expanded form

Many expressions can be written either in factored form, where the factors are shown prior to the multiplication, or in expanded form, which shows the completed multiplication.

Factored form	Expanded form
$3(x + 5)$	$3x + 15$

The distributive property helps us simplify equations and expressions that contain variables.

Use the distributive property to write the following expressions in expanded form:

$6(x + 2)$ and $3(7 - x)$.

A diagram of each expression can be used to help write the expanded form.

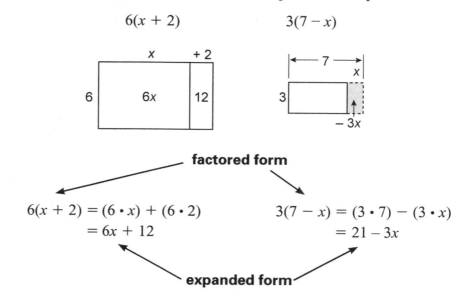

$6(x + 2)$ $3(7 - x)$

factored form

$6(x + 2) = (6 \cdot x) + (6 \cdot 2)$ $3(7 - x) = (3 \cdot 7) - (3 \cdot x)$
$\qquad = 6x + 12$ $\qquad = 21 - 3x$

expanded form

4. In countries other than the United States, the end zones of Ultimate fields are shorter. Metric measures are used to describe the dimensions of these fields.

   a) Write an expression for the length of the international Ultimate field shown below using x to represent the length of the end zones in meters.

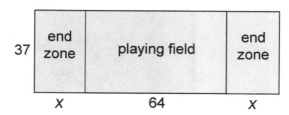

   b) Write an expression for the area of this field. Expand the expression using the distributive property.

   c) If the total area of both end zones is 1,332 m², how long is each end zone?

5. Many sports have rectangular fields or playing surfaces. For each court or field shown:

- Write an expression for the area.

- Expand the expression using the distributive property.

- Find the missing value and give the dimensions of the court or field.

a) NCAA and High School Basketball Courts: Area = 4,200 ft.^{2}

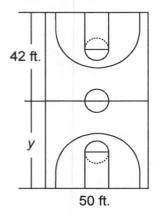

b) Tennis Doubles Court: Area = 2,808 ft.^{2}

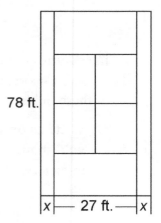

c) Field Hockey Field: Area = 54,000 ft.^{2}

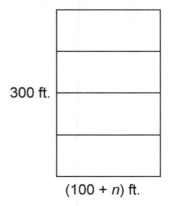

d) Badminton Singles Court: Area = 748 ft.²

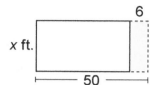

MATHEMATICALLY
SPEAKING

▶ term
▶ like terms

A term is one component in a sum that consists of a number, a variable, or the product of a number and one or more variables. The expression $xy - \frac{4}{x} + 9$ is made up of three terms, xy, $\frac{4}{x}$, and 9. Terms that have the same variables raised to the same powers are called like terms. For example, in the expression $2y + 5y$, the terms $2y$ and $5y$ are like terms.

When an expression contains like terms, you can simplify it by combining like terms. You can think of this process as the reverse of the distributive property.

$$2y + y = 2y + 1y \qquad 50x - 6x = x(50 - 6)$$
$$= y(2 + 1) \qquad\qquad = 44x$$
$$= 3y$$

You cannot simplify the expressions $6x + 12$ or $3x - 21$ as their terms are not alike.

Equivalent Expressions

MATHEMATICALLY
SPEAKING

▶ equivalent
  expressions

Sometimes two or more expressions are equivalent—they represent the same situation or mathematical relationship, using different combinations of numbers and symbols. For example, $29 + 387$ and $30 + 386$ are equivalent expressions, as are $3x + 7x$ and $2x + 8x$. When you expand an expression or when you combine like terms, the resulting expression is equivalent to the original. You can show that expressions are equivalent by using the equal sign.

$$35(x - 2) = 35x - 70 \qquad\qquad -6y + 10y + 3 = 4y + 3$$

6. The Nichols and Pevear families live in Chicago and always attend opening days at the two ballparks together. There are five people in the Nichols family and four people in the Pevear family. They purchase their tickets through Ticket Express, which charges a flat fee of $2 per ticket in addition to each ticket's cost.

   a) If *x* equals the price of an opening day ticket in the bleacher section, write two different expressions for the total cost the two families will pay for tickets.

   b) Explain in words why the expressions are equivalent.

   c) Opening day tickets to the Chicago Cubs cost $35 each, while opening day tickets to the Chicago White Sox cost $20 each. What is the cost for the group to attend the opening day for each of these teams?

rap It Up _____

Explain to a friend how you used the distributive property to solve the baseball problem above. What is important to know about the distributive property of multiplication over addition?

MATHEMATICALLY SPEAKING

▶ distributive property of multiplication over addition

▶ distributive property of multiplication over subtraction

▶ equivalent expressions

▶ expanded form

▶ factored form

▶ like terms

▶ term

Write About It

1. What are equivalent expressions? Give three examples. Make sure that one of your examples uses the distributive property.

2. Simplify the following expressions to form equivalent expressions. Underline additive inverses or multiplicative inverses.

   a) $8s + 13 - 8s + 7$

   b) $\left(-\frac{2}{9}\right)(81)\left(-\frac{9}{2}\right)$

   c) $\frac{1}{2}m + 11 - 11 - \frac{1}{2}m$

   d) $g + (-g) + \frac{1}{12} \cdot 12$

   e) $x + 3 + 9 + (-3)$

   f) $8 \cdot \frac{4}{7} \cdot \frac{1}{8}$

3. Dividing by a number is equivalent to multiplying by the reciprocal of that number. For example, dividing a number by 4 is the same as multiplying that number by $\frac{1}{4}$. Rewriting division as multiplication can make equations with variables easier to work with. Rewrite the following division expressions as equivalent multiplication expressions. Then, simplify.

   a) $72 \div 8$

   b) $-24 \div \frac{1}{4}$

   c) $(6 + 3) \div 9$

   d) $5x \div \frac{5}{6}$

   e) $(m \div 8) + 3$

   f) $\frac{7}{6}x \div 14$

   g) $(4 - y) \div 3$

   h) $s \div {}^-2$

4. Subtracting a number is the same as adding its additive inverse. For example, subtracting $5x$ is the same as adding the additive inverse of $5x$, which is $-5x$. Rewrite the subtraction expressions below as equivalent addition expressions. Then, simplify.

   a) $8w - 14w$

   b) $\frac{7}{9}x - (-1)$

   c) $-4 - (-7)$

   d) $-8x - 10x$

5. Simplify by combining like terms.

   a) $4x + 7 + 3x - 5$

   b) $\frac{2}{3}y + 15 + (-2) - y$

   c) $6m + 2n + (-3n) + 3m$

   d) $2x + 5 - 5x$

6. Use the distributive property to find the areas. Show all your steps.

a)
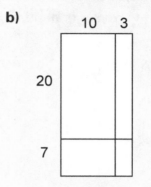

b)

10 3

20

7

7. Write expressions for the following situations. Then rewrite each expression in expanded form using the distributive property.

a) the product of 7 and the sum of 8 and x

b) the sum of 5 and p, multiplied by -2

c) five-sixths of the sum of -4 and 12

8. Write an equation to represent the following problem: The sum of two consecutive numbers is 35. What are the two numbers?

 **Hint**
See page 157

9. Write an equation to find the value of y (the length from each side of the volleyball court to the center) if the court's area is 1,800 square feet. How long is the volleyball court?

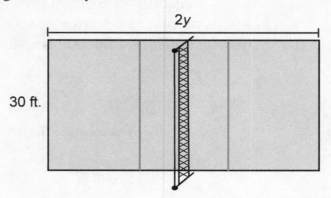

2y

30 ft.

10. Simplify these expressions by combining like terms.

    a) $4y + 7 + {}^{-}4y$ c) $\frac{2}{3}x + \frac{1}{2}x$

    b) $9p - 3w + 8w - 10p$ d) $16 - 6m + 2$

11. A theater sells tickets for a show. The box office charges an additional $3 service fee for each ticket purchased on the Internet.

    a) Write an expression for the cost of six tickets purchased on the Internet. Let p represent the price of one ticket.

    b) Write another expression for the cost of six tickets. Make sure one of your equivalent expressions uses parentheses and the other does not.

    c) Find the total cost of the tickets if each ticket costs $44.

12. During track practice, Jaclyn runs from the middle school to the local high school, runs one lap around the track, and then runs back to the middle school. It is 650 meters to the high school and x meters around the track. Write two equivalent expressions for the total distance in meters Jaclyn runs during five days of practice.

13. Examine the calculations below. Indicate where the following properties were applied: commutative property of multiplication, associative property of multiplication and distributive property of multiplication over addition.

Hint
See page 157

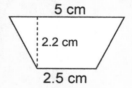

$$
\begin{aligned}
A_{\text{trapezoid}} &= \tfrac{1}{2}(b_1 + b_2)h \\
&= \tfrac{1}{2}(2.5 + 5)(2.2) \\
&= 1.1(2.5 + 5) \\
&= (1.1 \cdot 2.5) + (1.1 \cdot 5) \\
&= 2.75 + 5.5 \\
&= 8.25
\end{aligned}
$$

Think Beyond

14. Use properties to justify that 0.4, 0.40 and 0.400 are equivalent decimal values.

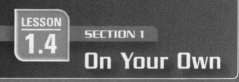

 Think Back

15. **a)** In one week at his summer job, Jonathan made $265.65. Jonathan's boss pays him $7.70 for each hour he works. Write an equation that can be used to find the number of hours Jonathan worked that week.

    b) Find the time Jonathan worked. Write this amount in "hours:minutes" format.

16. Find and fix the mistake in Lucy's work.

    $$17 - (^-3) \div (^-3) + \tfrac{2}{3} =$$
    $$(20) \div (^-3) + \tfrac{2}{3} =$$
    $$-\tfrac{20}{3} + \tfrac{2}{3} = {}^-6$$

17. List three numbers that are between 1.541 and 1.542.

18. Can two lines in the same plane be both parallel *and* perpendicular? Justify your answer using words or a drawing.

19. When you multiply two decimal numbers that are each less than 1 but greater than 0 (for example, 0.4 • 0.7), is the product always greater than each factor, less than each factor or between the factors? Explain.

 **Optional Technology Lesson for this section available in your eBook**

Sum It Up

Algebra lets us represent situations and relationships by combining numbers and letters in expressions, equations and inequalities.

- Expressions are mathematical combinations of numbers, letters and operations. An expression does not have an equal sign.

- An equation uses an equal sign ($=$) to tell us that two expressions are equivalent or equal.

- An inequality uses the symbols $>$ (greater than), $<$ (less than), $\geq$ (greater than or equal to) or $\leq$ (less than or equal to) to tell us how two expressions relate to each other.

- Variables are letters or symbols that can represent different values depending on the situation or the type of algebraic statement.

Meaning of Variables	
Specific unknown value	$n + 6 = 17$ $n = 11$
Related varying quantities	$y = 3x$ Coordinate pairs such as (0, 0), (−1, −3), (8, 24) and $\left(\frac{1}{2}, \frac{3}{2}\right)$ are part of the solution set.
Many values	$m \cdot 1 = m$ m can be any real number.

- Formulas are general mathematical rules that frequently involve measures such as perimeter, area, volume and distance. In many formulas, variables relate varying quantities.

$$C = \pi d \qquad V = lwh \qquad A = \tfrac{1}{2}bh$$

- Properties are general mathematical statements that use variables to generalize the behavior of certain sets of numbers. These variables can stand for many values. The following properties are true for any real numbers a, b and c.

Properties about the Order of Numbers	
commutative property of addition	Example: $a + b = b + a$ $^-16 + 4 = 4 + {}^-16$
commutative property of multiplication	Example: $a \cdot b = b \cdot a$ $5 \cdot \frac{3}{4} = \frac{3}{4} \cdot 5$
Properties about the Grouping of Numbers	
associative property of addition	$a + (b + c) = (a + b) + c$ Example: $3.1 + (2.9 + 8.7) = (3.1 + 2.9) + 8.7$
associative property of multiplication	$(a \cdot b) \cdot c = a \cdot (b \cdot c)$ Example: $(7 \cdot 9) \cdot 20 = 7 \cdot (9 \cdot 20)$
Important Properties Involving 0 and 1	
additive inverse	$a + {}^-a = 0 \qquad {}^-a + a = 0$ Example: $5 + {}^-5 = 0 \qquad {}^-8.3 + 8.3 = 0$
multiplicative inverse	$a \cdot \frac{1}{a} = 1 \qquad \frac{1}{a} \cdot a = 1$ Example: $6 \cdot \frac{1}{6} = 1 \qquad \frac{1}{6} \cdot 6 = 1$
identity property of addition	$a + 0 = a \qquad 0 + a = a$ Example: $^-2 + 0 = {}^-2 \qquad 0 + {}^-2 = {}^-2$
identity property of multiplication	$a \cdot 1 = a \qquad 1 \cdot a = a$ Example: $24 \cdot 1 = 24 \qquad 1 \cdot 24 = 24$
Properties Involving Two Operations	
distributive property of multiplication over addition	$a(b + c) = ab + ac$ Example: $8(x + 3) = 8x + 24$
	$(b + c)a = ba + ca$ Example: $(^-2 + 7)n = {}^-2n + 7n$
distributive property of multiplication over subtraction	$a(b - c) = ab - ac$ Example: $12(m - 1) = 12m - 12$
	$(b - c)a = ba - ca$ Example: $\left(\frac{1}{2} - w\right)3 = \frac{3}{2} - 3w$

MATHEMATICALLY SPEAKING

Do you know what these mathematical terms mean?

- additive inverse
- associative property of addition
- associative property of multiplication
- commutative property of addition
- commutative property of multiplication
- constant
- distributive property of multiplication over addition

- distributive property of multiplication over subtraction
- equation
- equivalent expressions
- evaluate (an expression)
- expanded form
- expression
- factored form
- formula
- identity element

- identity property of addition
- identity property of multiplication
- inequality
- like terms
- multiplicative inverses
- solution
- solve (an equation)
- term
- variable

Part 1. What did you learn?

1. Fill in the blanks in the following paragraph: Bob's teacher asked him to simplify the _____ 4(22.5). Bob used the
   _____ to create the _____ expression 4(22) +
   ₂   ₃
   4(0.5). The expression 4(22) + 4(0.5) can be _____ to
   ₄
   equal 90.

2. In each of the following expressions or equations, determine if
   m represents one specific value, related varying quantities, many
   values or something else.

   a. Lara's little sister is $2m$ tall.

   b. $m + 44 = 100$

   c. $5 \cdot m \cdot 2 = 10 \cdot m$

   d. $4 + 3m$

3. Match each phrase to a mathematical expression. In each case,
   let *x* represent the number of songs on an MP3 player.

a. 3 more than the product of 6 and x	**e.** $x - 6$
b. 3 times the sum of 6 and x	**f.** $x + 6$
c. 6 less than x	**g.** $6x + 3$
d 6 more than x	**h.** $3(6 + x)$

4. Graph the values that make $x > {}^-3$ true when x is a real number.

5. Graph the values that make $4 + w < 4$ true when w is an integer.

6. Simplify these expressions to form equivalent expressions by
   grouping like terms together.

   a. $6w + 8 - 5w - 3$

   b. $8n + 2p + 7n + ({}^-2p)$

   c. $21a \cdot \frac{1}{3}$

   d. $10x - 5 - 12x + 10$

7. Bobbie's soccer coach told him to drink six 8-ounce glasses of water a day. Bobbie's water is sold in liter bottles. For approximation purposes, one liter is about 32 fluid ounces.

   a. Approximately how many liters of water should Bobbie be drinking each day? How do you know?

   b. Bobbie's water is sold by the case. The total capacity of a case is 12 liters. Approximately how many days' supply of water does Bobbie have if he buys one case?

   c. Write a formula that could be used to convert from liters to fluid ounces. Define your variables.

8. The formula $A = \pi r^2$ is used to find the area of a circle. Use the formula to find the area of each of the following sizes of pizza. (Use 3.14 for π.)

   a. A 6-inch pizza ($r = 3$ in.)

   b. A 12-inch pizza ($r = 6$ in.)

   c. A 16-inch pizza ($r = 8$ in.)

   d. Based on your calculations in Parts a and b, should a 12-inch pizza cost twice as much as a 6-inch pizza? Why or why not?

9. Write an expression for the area of each rectangle using the distributive property. Then, expand your expressions and simplify. Show all of your steps.

   a.

   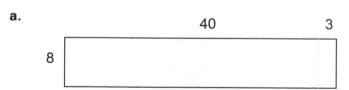

   b.

   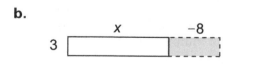

10. A sketch of the soccer field at Foster Elementary school is shown below. The total area of the field is 2,400 square feet.

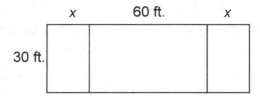

x   60 ft.   x

30 ft.

   a. Use the distributive property to write an expression equivalent to the area.

   b. Expand the expression.

   c. Find the missing value and give the dimensions of the field.

11. Write an equation where changing the order of the numbers makes the computations easier. Which property allows you to change the order of the numbers in your equation?

12. Each equation in Column A has started to be simplified in order to make the computation simpler to perform mentally. Match each equation in Column A with the property (or properties) in Column B that is/are used to simplify the equation. Then, find the simplified value of the expression in Column C.

Column A	Column B	Column C
(a) $(-0.4 + 15.1) + 4.9 = -0.4 + (15.1 + 4.9)$	**(f)** Additive Inverses	**(k)** 3
(b) $4.5 \cdot 8 = (4 \cdot 8) + (0.5 \cdot 8)$	**(g)** Multiplicative Inverses	**(l)** 4
(c) $12 \cdot \left(1\frac{1}{3} \cdot \frac{1}{4}\right) = \left(12 \cdot 1\frac{1}{3}\right) \cdot \frac{1}{4}$	**(h)** Associative Property of Addition	**(m)** 340
(d) $43 + 297 = 43 + (-3) + 297 + (3)$	**(i)** Associative Property of Multiplication	**(n)** 36
(e) $4\frac{1}{2} \cdot \frac{2}{3} = \left(4\frac{1}{2} \cdot 2\right) \cdot \left(\frac{2}{3} \cdot \frac{1}{2}\right)$	**(j)** Distributive Property of Multiplication Over Addition	**(o)** 19.6

13. Find the value of n in each equation mentally.

    a. $\frac{1}{4} + n + \frac{3}{4} = 2\frac{3}{4}$

    b. $2.5n + 12 - 12 - 0.5n = 20$

    c. $11.8 + n + 0.2 = 15$

    d. $\left(\frac{3}{4}\right)(n)\left(\frac{4}{3}\right) = 12$

    e. $\frac{(5 \cdot 3 \cdot 4)}{(4 \cdot n \cdot 5)} = 1$

    f. Choose one of the equations above and show or explain which property you used to solve it mentally.

14. Evaluate the expression $12 + 2x$ for each of the specified values.

    a. $x = {}^-3.5$

    b. $x = \frac{1}{2}$

    c. $x = 2.5$

15. Evaluate the expression $20 - 4.5x$ for each of the specified values.

    a. $x = {}^-2$

    b. $x = 10$

    c. $x = 0$

16. Taryn's teacher called the letter n in the equation $6 \cdot n = 24$ a variable. Taryn is confused because she thought variables represent many values and in this equation, n can only represent the number 4. Is n a variable in this number sentence? Why or why not?

17. Davio answered the following question on a recent quiz.

Which method below could **not** be used to find the area of a 6-inch by 48-inch rectangle?

A. $6(50) - 6(2)$ **C.** $6(40 + 8)$

B. $6(40) + 8$ **D.** $6(40) + 6(8)$

Davio chose answer A because he didn't think that subtraction could be used to find the area of a rectangle. Davio's answer was marked wrong. Explain why choice A is not the correct answer. Then, explain which answer is correct.

18. Monica's teacher asked her to simplify the expression $97 + 8 \cdot 3$. Monica said, "That's easy. I can make the computations easier by using the commutative properties and changing the order of the numbers." Here is what she did:

$97 + 8 \cdot 3 = 97 + 3 \cdot 8 = 100 \cdot 8 = 800$

What is wrong with Monica's reasoning? What doesn't she understand about the commutative properties of addition and multiplication?

Solving Equations

One reason mathematics is so powerful is that we can use symbols to model real situations. But we need to understand the meaning of the symbols we use and the way to find the values for these symbols. This section focuses on writing and solving equations.

 LESSON 2.1 Undoing Operations

 Start It Off

Look at the blocks below. Each stage has one more hexagon and two more rhombi than the stage before it.

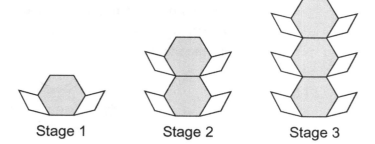

Stage 1   Stage 2   Stage 3

1. Draw Stage 4 and Stage 5.

2. Make a table that shows the stage number and the total number of blocks for the first eight stages.

3. Describe in words how the total number of blocks is changing from one stage to the next.

MATHEMATICALLY SPEAKING

▶ recursive (iterative) rule

You can use a recursive rule to find the number of blocks at any stage based on the number of blocks in the stage before it. In general, a recursive rule is a rule for finding a term in a sequence based on the previous term.

$$new = previous + constant$$

4. Write the recursive rule for finding the number of blocks at each stage using the words *new* and *previous*.

One useful idea in mathematics is that you can undo operations. Operations that undo each other, such as addition and subtraction, are called inverse operations. What other inverse operations do you know?

Many athletes work out at a gym where they lift weights and stretch. They follow a routine of exercises and then repeat the routine a few times. One Saturday morning, Clarence made a routine that included seven different exercises. Just before he began, his trainer added two more exercises. Clarence completed 12 repetitions of each exercise. He went through his complete routine three times. How many exercises did he perform on Saturday?

Flowcharts are useful tools for solving problems like this one. A flowchart starts with an input. It then indicates the operations to do to the input. It ends with an output. You follow the direction of the arrows in a flowchart.

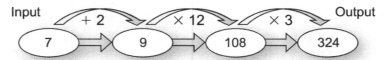

You can work backwards through a flowchart by undoing each operation—in other words, by using inverse operations. Start at the output and then do the inverse operations along each arrow. Follow the direction of the arrows toward the input.

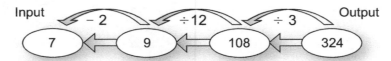

Look at the flowchart above. If you start with an output of 324, how can you use inverse operations to find the input?

I'm thinking of a number. If you subtract 7 from my number and then multiply the result by 2, you get −12. What is the number I'm thinking of?

You can model this problem by first making a flowchart that shows how to get from any input to the output. Then start with the given output of −12 and use inverse operations to work backwards through the flowchart and find the input.

Work backwards to find the mystery input number.

Step 1: −12 ÷ 2 = −6

Step 2: −6 + 7 = 1

Check: $(1 - 7) \cdot 2 = -12$

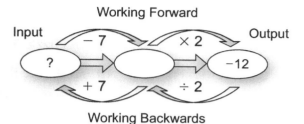

1. Make up a set of calculations and draw a flowchart to illustrate them. Show how to undo the operations on your flowchart.

2. Work with a partner. Copy each flowchart below. Fill in the missing values. Under each one, draw and label arrows to show the operations you would use to work backwards. Do not use a calculator.

   a)

   b)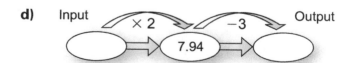

   c)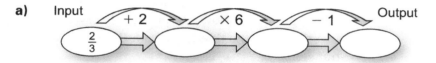

   d)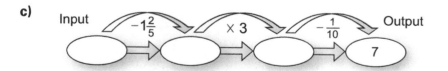

   e)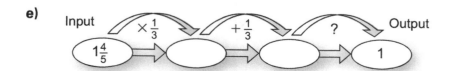

3. How can you check to see if your input value for Question 2c is correct? Show your work.

4. Create three flowchart puzzles like the ones in Question 2, using the criteria below. Each flowchart must have at least three different operations.

a) In Puzzle 1 use whole number operations.

b) In Puzzle 2 use fraction operations such as $+ \frac{1}{7}$.

c) In Puzzle 3 use decimal operations such as $\div 2.4$.

d) Exchange flowchart puzzles with a partner and solve to find the missing values.

 **W**rap It Up _____

Inverse operations and working backwards are useful when solving problems. How do you work backwards through a flowchart? Use the flowchart from Question 2e to illustrate your steps.

On Your Own

 Write About It

1. Give examples of inverse operations. Explain to a friend how flowcharts work. Then explain how to work backwards through a flowchart, undoing the operations, to solve a problem. Provide an example.

For Questions 2–5, copy and complete the flowcharts.

2.

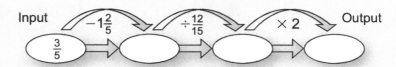

3.

4.

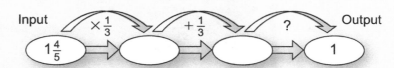

5.

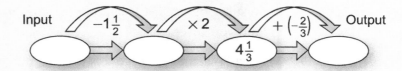

6. At the end of the school day, Ms. E. Quayshun, the mathematics teacher, had 17 pencils. She gave out 14 pencils in her morning class, and got 12 pencils back at lunchtime. She gave out 11 more pencils in her afternoon math class. How many pencils did Ms. E. Quayshun have at the start of the school day?

 **Hint**
See page 157

7. Christine bought a small box of whole walnuts. On her way home she ate half of the walnuts. At home she ate 4 more walnuts. There were 8 walnuts left. How many walnuts were in the box when Christine bought it? Use a flowchart to model the situation.

8. Working backwards is a technique that can be used to analyze games. Play the game of Nim a couple of times. Then devise a strategy that might help you win the game.

GAME · · · · · **Game of Nim** · · · · · · ·

Players: 2 people

DIRECTIONS:

Put 15 chips on the table. Players take turns. During a turn, the player removes one, two or three chips from the table. The player who takes the last chip(s) off the table wins the game.

9. Complete this flowchart in two different ways.

? Hint
See page 157

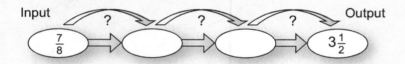

Input — ? — ? — ? — Output
$\frac{7}{8}$ — $3\frac{1}{2}$

10. I'm thinking of a number. If you multiply the number by 3 and add 4 to the result, you get 19. What number am I thinking of? Use a flowchart to help you solve.

Think Beyond

11. Make a flowchart to solve this number puzzle.

Gala McIntosh picked a basket of apples one afternoon. When a group of students arrived at the orchard, she gave away one-half of her apples. Later she gave one-half of the apples that were left to a group of senior citizens. She then ate 6 apples herself. If Ms. McIntosh has 3 apples left in her basket, how many apples did she start with?

12. What is the diameter of a circle that has a circumference of
265.33 meters? (Use 3.14 for π.)

    A. 9.2 meters   **C.** 42.25 meters

    B. 169 meters   **D.** 84.5 meters

13. **a)** Kyle said, "10% off of a $100.00 pair of sneakers means $10.00
off." After hearing this, Henry said, "20% off of a $150.00 pair of
sneakers should be $20.00." What is wrong with Henry's logic?

    b) What is 20% off of a $150.00 pair of sneakers?

14. Francis started her 150-square-foot flower garden last spring. The
garden was 5 feet wide and 30 feet long. This year, Francis is making
her garden 6 feet longer. Show how you can use the distributive
property to find the area of the new garden.

30 ft.

5 ft. ☐

30 ft.   6 ft.

5 ft. ☐

15. **a)** Determine if this statement is true or false. If the statement is
false, correct it.

$$\tfrac{1}{2} \cdot ☺ = ☺ \div 2$$

    b) What does ☺ represent?

16. **a)** Estimate each sum and explain your reasoning.

    b) Find the exact sum. Show your work.

      i) $4\tfrac{2}{5} + \left(-2\tfrac{6}{10}\right) = y$

      ii) $-0.778 + \tfrac{1}{4} = K$

LESSON 2.2 Solving Equations by Undoing

➡️ **Start It Off**

An explicit rule states the relationship between two sets of values. In Lesson 2.1, you wrote a recursive rule for the sequence below. To compute the number of blocks in a stage using this rule, you have to find the number of blocks at each of the previous stages. This can be time consuming for stages far along in the sequence. An explicit rule would allow you to calculate the number of blocks at any stage, without finding the numbers in the stages before.

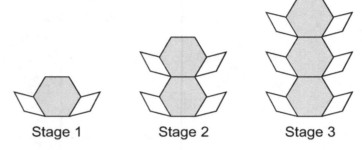

Stage 1   Stage 2   Stage 3

1. Find the explicit rule relating the stage number and the total number of blocks. Use n to represent the stage number and T to represent the total number of blocks.

2. Use the explicit rule and find the total number of blocks in Stage 18, Stage 39, and Stage 90.

3. Which stage in the pattern uses 42 blocks?

4. Describe how the number(s) in your explicit rule are connected to the sequence.

One Saturday, the Sands company of Wyoming put x rafts on the Snake River. Each raft was filled with 7 people. How many rafts were there if 35 people went rafting? This situation can be expressed as:

$$7x = 35$$

This equation uses multiplication: 7 times x equals 35. You might just know that $x = 5$ because $7 \cdot 5 = 35$. But what if you were solving an equation with numbers that were fractions or decimals? This lesson teaches you how to solve simple equations, regardless of the numbers used. You'll do this by using inverse operations and the "undoing method."

To begin, you must be able to identify the operations used in equations.

1. Examine the simple equations below and answer the following questions.

  a) What operation is being used in each equation?

  b) What inverse operation can be used to undo the specific operation?

  i) $w - 32 = {}^-14$

  ii) $4\frac{2}{5} + n = 8$

  iii) $^-5x = 42$

  iv) $\frac{m}{4} = 9$

Addition and Subtraction Equations

To undo an operation, you use the inverse operation. Flowcharts can help you choose the operation needed to undo the operation in a simple equation. Place the variable in the input oval. If the variable is not the first term in the equation, you may need to rearrange the symbols. Mathematicians show their steps when solving equations to keep a record of their work.

The inverse operations of addition and subtraction are used to solve equations with these operations.

Example 1

Solve $w - 32 = {}^-14$.

Flowchart

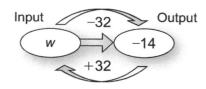

Solution Steps	**Explanation**
$w - 32 = {}^-14$	Original equation
$w = {}^-14 + 32$	Rewrite the equation to undo subtraction with addition.
$w = 18$	Perform calculation to determine w.
$18 - 32 \overset{?}{=} {}^-14$	Check by substitution.
$^-14 = {}^-14$	Correct

Example 2

Solve $4\frac{2}{5} + n = 8$.

First change the order of the addends using the commutative property:
$n + 4\frac{2}{5} = 8$

Flowchart

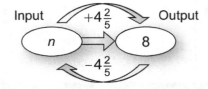

Input $+4\frac{2}{5}$ Output

n 8

$-4\frac{2}{5}$

Solution Steps	Explanation
$n + 4\frac{2}{5} = 8$	Original equation
$n = 8 - 4\frac{2}{5}$	Rewrite the equation to undo addition with subtraction.
$n = 3\frac{3}{5}$	Perform calculation to determine n.
$3\frac{3}{5} + 4\frac{2}{5} \overset{?}{=} 8$	Check by substitution.
$8 = 8$	Correct

2. Solve the equations below. Show your solution steps. You may want to draw flowcharts.

a) $25 = n + (^-31)$ **d)** $q - 84 = 13$

b) $c - (^-27) = ^-1\frac{3}{4}$ **e)** $m + ^-3.8 = 9.21$

c) $-\frac{7}{8} + k = ^-1\frac{1}{2}$ **f)** $5 = x - (^-1)$

Multiplication and Division Equations

You can also use flowcharts and undoing operations to solve simple multiplication or division equations. Some equations, such as the rafting example, $7x = 35$, are easy to solve mentally. But the solutions to most equations are not obvious. Examine the following:

Example 3

Solve $-5y = 42$.

Flowchart

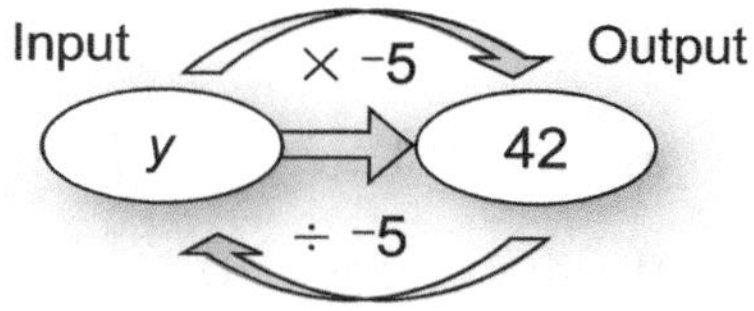

Input   × -5 Output

y → 42

÷ -5

Solution Steps	Explanation
$-5y = 42$	Original equation
$y = 42 \div -5$	Rewrite the equation to undo multiplication with division.
$y = -8.4$	Perform calculation to determine y.
$-5(-8.4) \overset{?}{=} 42$	Check by substitution.
$42 = 42$	Correct

Example 4

Solve $\frac{m}{4} = 9$.

Flowchart

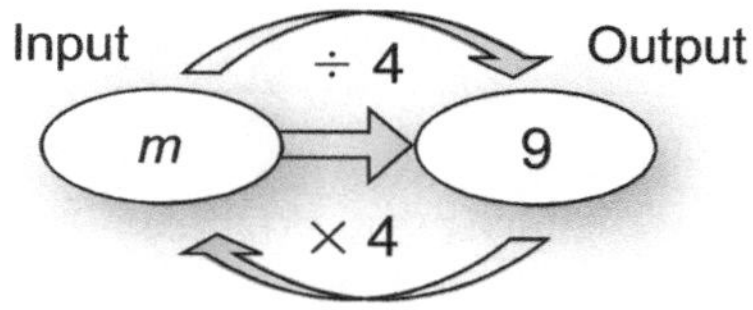

Input   ÷ 4 Output

m → 9

× 4

Solution Steps	Explanation
$\frac{m}{4} = 9$	Original equation
$m = 9 \cdot 4$	Rewrite the equation to undo division with multiplication.
$m = 36$	Perform calculation to determine m.
$\frac{36}{4} \overset{?}{=} 9$	Check by substitution.
$9 = 9$	Correct

3. Recording the steps when you solve equations helps you keep a record of your actions and thoughts. Solve these equations, recording your steps. You may want to make a flowchart to help you decide on the undoing operation.

   a) $\frac{n}{7} = 28$

   b) $16 = (^-3)c$

   c) $m \div 6 = \frac{1}{12}$

   d) $2 = \frac{3}{5}n$

   e) $^-6 = 1.8y$

   f) $4(x + 1) = 20$

4. How do you decide which operation to use to solve an equation?

5. Not all equations are easily solved by undoing the operation. Discuss with your partner how to solve $^-7 - n = 10$.

 **Wrap It Up**

What mathematical ideas are important to understand if you are going to solve equations by undoing operations? Make a list and define them in your own words.

MATHEMATICALLY SPEAKING

▶ explicit rule

LESSON
2.2　**SECTION 2**

On Your Own

 Write
About It

1. Drawing a flowchart every time you want to solve an equation takes time. Give another student hints on how to find the operation to use to solve an equation without having to draw a flowchart. Use an example to show your ideas.

2. Some multiplication and division equations use negative numbers. How do you know whether a solution will be negative or positive? Give four examples that show all the possible combinations.

3. Westcoast Biking Company runs bicycle trips for teenagers. Below are the costs per student to go on one of Westcoast's trips.

   • $85 for each bike rental

   • $225 for food and camping

   Let n represent the number of teenagers. Write equations for the following and solve:

   a) The total bicycle rental cost was $1,105. How many teens needed bikes?

   b) On one trip, Westcoast collected $3,825 for food and camping. How many teenagers went on that bike trip?

4. Solve the following equations using inverse operations. Record your steps.

   a) $n - 17 = 3.6$

   b) $15 = x + {}^-2\frac{1}{3}$

   c) $8 = y - ({}^-1)$

   d) $1\frac{5}{8} + s = 4$

5. Solve the following equations. Record your steps.

   a) $42k = 100$

   b) $\frac{2}{7}w = 8$

   c) $^-3g = 5\frac{1}{4}$

   d) $n \div 2\frac{1}{2} = 12$

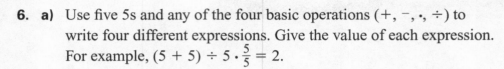
6. a) Use five 5s and any of the four basic operations $(+, -, \cdot, \div)$ to write four different expressions. Give the value of each expression. For example, $(5 + 5) \div 5 \cdot \frac{5}{5} = 2$.

 Hint
See page 157

 **Think Beyond**

b) Use five 5s and any of the operations in any combination to form expressions that have a value of 1, 2, 3, 4, 5, ...10.

7. Solve the following equations by undoing the operations.

a) $-11 = a - (-7)$

b) $-\frac{3}{4} + p = 4$

c) $d - 24.3 = -2.8$

d) $-9 = m + -2\frac{1}{3}$

8. Petra had $85.50 after she bought a calculator. The calculator cost $94.34 including tax.

a) Write an equation for this situation. Let y represent the amount of money Petra had before her purchase.

b) How much money did Petra have before buying the calculator?

9. Solve the following equations. If there is no real number solution, write that.

a) $7|x| = 21$

b) $|x| \div 4 = 3.6$

c) $2|x| = -10$

 **Think Beyond**

10. Toby is making guacamole for a party. Avocados cost $1.89 each. She wants to spend $15 on avocados.

a) Write an equation to find the number of avocados Toby can buy.

b) Solve your equation. How many avocados can Toby buy?

Think Beyond

11. In this lesson you learned to solve simple, one-step equations using inverse operations. But certain equations require more than one step when undoing. Explore how to solve the following equations. Come up with a general way that will work for other equations similar to these.

a) $3 \div n = 8$ **b)** $-52 - n = 4\frac{1}{4}$

12. Simplify $\frac{432}{468}$.

13. A regular hexagon has a side length of 3.65 cm. What is the perimeter of the hexagon?

14. Explain how to solve this equation using mental math: $\frac{4}{5} + x = 1\frac{1}{5}$.

15. After dinner at a restaurant, the waiter brings you the check. The dinner is $28.71. Which of the following is the best estimate of a 20% tip?

   A. $20.00   C. $57.42

   B. $6.00   D. $4.00

16. Evaluate if $m = -2$: $-12m + (-12) - m$.

LESSON 2.3 Solving Equations Using Balance

 Start It Off

Look at the sequence below. Each stage has one more square than the stage before it.

  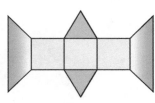

| Stage 1 | Stage 2 | Stage 3 |

1. Sketch Stages 4 and 5.

2. What part of the design remains constant and what part varies with each stage?

3. Make a table with the stage number and the total number of blocks for the first six stages.

4. Find the recursive rule for finding the number of blocks in each stage of this sequence.

5. What would Stage 0 look like? Sketch Stage 0.

There are a number of ways to solve equations, and one of them involves the idea of balance. It is important to master this "balancing method" because you can use it to solve all types of equations.

Skateboarding is a popular sport. One skateboard trick, the "ollie," was invented in 1976 by Alan "Ollie" Gelfand. It involves the skateboard and rider becoming airborne. Danny Wainwright holds the world record for the highest ollie. He jumped 44.5 inches in 2000. The length of time from the invention of the ollie to when Danny Wainwright set the world record can be found by solving for x in the equation $1976 + x = 2000$.

The Balancing Method: Additive Inverses and Equality

Balance scales help to explain the balance method. The main idea is that when you add the same amount of weight to both pans of a balance scale, the scale stays balanced. Likewise, when you add the same values to the expressions on both sides of an equal sign in an equation, the expressions remain equal.

How do you decide what number or variable to add to both sides of the equation? Usually you add the additive inverse of the number that is added to the variable.

Example 1

How many years after the ollie was invented did Danny Wainwright jump 44.5 inches? To help you understand the balance method, we'll first show the solution using a pan balance. Solve the equation $1976 + x = 2000$.

· Represent the equation with a balance scale to understand how the balancing method works.

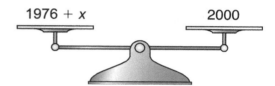

• Balance the scale by adding the same amount, $^-1976$, to both pans. The additive inverse of 1976 is $^-1976$.

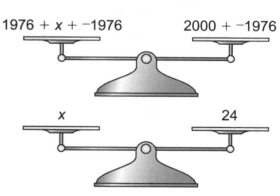

• Use symbols and the balancing method to find the value of x.

$$1976 + x = 2000$$ Original equation

$$1976 + x + {^-1976} = 2000 + {^-1976}$$ Add the additive inverse of 1976 to both sides of the equal sign to maintain balance.

$$x + 0 = 24$$ $1976 + {^-1976} = 0$

$$x = 24$$ Simplify. Perform calculation to determine x.

The ollie record was set 24 years after the invention of the ollie.

$$1976 + 24 \overset{?}{=} 2000$$ Check by substitution.

$$2000 = 2000$$ Correct

In the equation $1976 + x = 2000$, the variable x is in the expression $1976 + x$. You want to add a number to this expression that will leave you with x alone. To do this you add the additive inverse of 1976, which is $^-1976$. The resulting expression simplifies to $0 + x$, or x. But to keep everything balanced, you must also add $^-1976$ to the other side. When you add the same amount to either side of an equal sign, you are using the addition property of equality.

Does this balancing method work with subtraction equations? It does, but first change the subtraction sentence to an equivalent addition sentence.

Example 2

Carrie bought a new skateboard. She paid $97.95 for it and had $8.50 left over. How much money did Carrie have before buying her new skateboard?

Represent this situation with the equation $m - 97.95 = 8.50$.

Represent the equation with a balance scale to understand how the balancing method works.

- Rewrite the subtraction as an addition: $m + (^-97.95) = 8.50$.

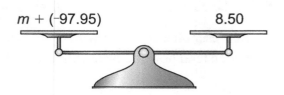

- Balance the scale by adding the same amount, 97.95, to both pans. The additive inverse of $^-97.95$ is 97.95.

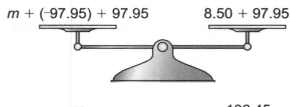

- Use symbols and the balancing method to find the value of m.

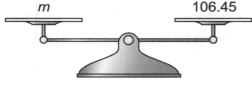

$m - 97.95 = 8.50$	Original equation
$m + (^-97.95) = 8.50.$	Subtracting 97.95 is equivalent to adding the opposite of 97.95.
$m + (^-97.95) + 97.95 = 8.50 + 97.95$	Add the additive inverse of $^-97.95$ to both sides.
$m + 0 = 106.45$	$^-97.95 + 97.95 = 0$
$m = 106.45$	Simplify.

Carrie had $106.45 before buying a new skateboard.

$106.45 - 97.95 \overset{?}{=} 8.50$	Check by substitution.
$8.50 = 8.50$	Correct

1. Solve the equations using the balancing method. Record your steps.

a) $m + 18 = 13$

b) $1.4 + n = 9$

c) $32 = -6 + a$

d) $y - (-1) = -5$

e) $20 = x - 7$

f) $b - 5 = \frac{3}{4}$

Leanne and Crystal, two middle school students, each found a different way to use the balancing method to solve an equation. Examine the equation $25 - d = -8$. Before reading the example, discuss with a partner how you might solve it using the balancing method.

Example 3

Leanne solved the equation, $25 - d = -8$, using the following method.

Crystal used a different set of steps to solve $25 - d = -8$.

> I added the opposite of 25 to each side of the equal sign. I ended up with -d = -33. My teacher said to multiply both sides of the equation by -1 but I'm not sure why.

> First, I added the opposite of d to both sides. I got 25 = -8 + d. Then I added the opposite of -8 to both sides. I found that d = 33.

$$25 - d = -8$$
$$25 + {}^-d = -8$$
$$25 + {}^-25 + {}^-d = -8 + {}^-25$$
$$0 + {}^-d = -33$$
$${}^-d = -33$$
$${}^-d \cdot {}^-1 = -33 \cdot {}^-1$$
$$d = 33$$

$$25 - 33 \overset{?}{=} -8 \quad \text{Check by substitution.}$$
$$-8 = -8 \quad \text{Correct}$$

$$25 - d = -8$$
$$25 + {}^-d = -8$$
$$25 + d + {}^-d = -8 + d$$
$$25 + 0 = -8 + d$$
$$25 = -8 + d$$
$$25 + 8 = -8 + 8 + d$$
$$33 = 0 + d$$
$$33 = d$$

$$25 - 33 \overset{?}{=} -8 \quad \text{Check by substitution.}$$
$$-8 = -8 \quad \text{Correct}$$

2. **a)** Explain Leanne's steps.

   b) Explain Crystal's steps. Which approach would you use? Why?

3. Solve the equations using the balancing method. Check your answers.

   a) $5 - m = 30$

   b) $3\frac{1}{2} - y = \frac{5}{8}$

   c) $^-62 - x = 10$

The Balancing Method: Multiplicative Inverses and Equality

What are the effects of multiplying the weights on both pans of a balance scale by the same amount? Just like when you added the same amount to each pan, the scale stays balanced. Similarly, when you multiply the expressions on each side of the equal sign in an equation by the same number, the expressions remain equal. We can use this idea to solve certain types of equations. When you multiply both sides of an equation by the same amount, you are using the multiplication property of equality.

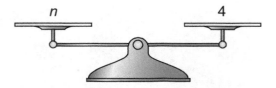
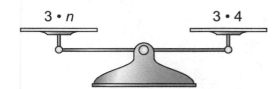

Consider the equation $16h = {}^-56$. As with addition equations, to solve this equation, we want to get the variable h alone on one side. To do this, we can multiply $16h$ by $\frac{1}{16}$, the reciprocal of 16. We also have to multiply $^-56$ by $\frac{1}{16}$ to maintain the balance.

Example 4

Solve $16h = {}^-56$.

$$16h = {}^-56 \qquad \text{Original equation}$$

$$\frac{1}{16} \cdot 16h = \frac{1}{16} \cdot {}^-56 \qquad \text{Multiply by } \frac{1}{16}, \text{ the reciprocal of 16.}$$

$$1 \cdot h = {}^-3.5 \qquad \frac{1}{16} \cdot 16 = 1.$$

$$h = {}^-3\frac{1}{2} \qquad \text{Simplify.}$$

$$16\left({}^-3\frac{1}{2}\right) \overset{?}{=} {}^-56 \qquad \text{Check by substitution.}$$

$$^-56 = {}^-56 \qquad \text{Correct}$$

Example 5

Solve $\frac{x}{8} = 3.4$.

$\frac{x}{8} = 3.4$ Original equation

$\frac{1}{8} \cdot x = 3.4$ Rewrite the left side as a multiplication expression.

$8 \cdot \frac{1}{8} \cdot x = 8 \cdot 3.4$ Multiply both sides by 8, the reciprocal of $\frac{1}{8}$.

$1 \cdot x = 27.2$ $8 \cdot \frac{1}{8} = 1$

$x = 27.2$ Simplify.

$\frac{27.2}{8} \overset{?}{=} 3.4$ Check by substitution.

$3.4 = 3.4$ Correct

4. a) Why in Example 5 can you write $\frac{1}{8} \cdot x = 3.4$?

    b) Why is each side of the equation multiplied by 8?

Tom and Jasmine are discussing how they solved $\frac{12}{m} = 4$.

Why does it work to multiply both sides of the equation by m and then by $\frac{1}{4}$?

I first multiplied each side of the equation by m. I then multiplied both sides by $\frac{1}{4}$.

5. a) Here are the steps that Tom recorded. Explain each of the steps in Tom's solution.

$$\frac{12}{m} = 4$$

$$m \cdot \frac{12}{m} = 4 \cdot m$$

$$12 = 4m$$

$$\frac{1}{4} \cdot 12 = 4m \cdot \frac{1}{4}$$

$$3 = m$$

b) What are m and $\frac{1}{m}$ called?

c) Answer Jasmine's question, "Why does it work to multiply both sides of the equation by m and then by $\frac{1}{4}$?"

6. Practice using the balancing method to solve these equations. Check your answers.

a) $-29 = -7x$

c) $\frac{3}{4}c = 6$

b) $\frac{a}{4} = 0.003$

d) $-\frac{3}{w} = 15$

Wrap It Up

The balancing method is another way to solve equations. Compare this method to the undoing method. Use the following examples, $-\frac{3}{4}x = 21$ and $-7 - x = 3$, to compare and contrast the two methods.

MATHEMATICALLY SPEAKING

▶ addition property of equality

▶ multiplication property of equality

Write
About It

Check all your solutions by substituting your answer into the original equation.

1. One approach to solving equations is to use a balancing method. Explain how to solve the following equations using this method.

    a) $-5.2 + m = 14$

    b) $\frac{n}{9} = 0.8$

2. Alecia babysits on weekends and gets $7.50 per hour. During spring vacation week, she made $240. Write an equation you could solve to find the number of hours Alecia babysat during spring vacation. Be sure to define your variables. Solve your equation to find the number of hours she worked during vacation.

3. Evaluate the following using the order of operations.

    Hint
    See page 157

    a) $-2(5 + 6) + 7 \cdot 3$

    b) $\dfrac{4(5 + 3) + 3}{2(3) - 1}$

    c) $11 \cdot 4 + {-10} \cdot 3$

    d) $(4 - 9)^2 + 11 - 7 \div 2$

4. Write each word statement in symbols.

    a) twelve times a number

    b) the difference between a number and six

    c) four added to a number

    d) the product of eight and nine less than a number

    e) a number subtracted from twenty-one

    f) two-thirds of a number

    g) six times the sum of a number plus five

    h) the product of two and three more than a number

5. Ace Copiers charges $0.03 per copy. The student council at Milburn Middle School plans to advertise their fund-raiser by distributing flyers. If they have $50, how many flyers can they have copied?

6. Solve the following equations using the balancing method.

Hint
See page 157

   a) $25 - y = 10$

   b) $^-18 + y = 24$

   c) $6 + y = 1.2$

   d) $y - 4 = \frac{3}{4}$

7. **a)** The Downtown Deli is running a fund-raiser. They decide to give 5¢ for every dollar they make on a busy Saturday to the National Heart Association. Write an equation to represent this situation.

   b) What do the variables represent in your equation?

   c) If the deli makes $564, how much will they donate to the National Heart Association?

8. Examine the following equations. Simplify them if possible by combining like terms and expanding. Indicate if there are no real solutions or an infinite number of solutions.

Hint
See page 157

   a) $41 - 3x = 41 + {}^-3x$

   b) $7(2 + m) = 7(2) + m$

   c) $4(n + 1) = (n + 1) + (n + 1) + (n + 1) + (n + 1)$

   d) $m - ({}^-5) = {}^-m + ({}^-5)$

   e) $j + {}^-1 = j$

9. Trisha drew the following flowchart for $n \div \frac{3}{4} = 6$. Pedro thinks the flowchart is incorrect.

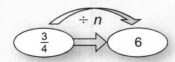

   a) Do you agree with Pedro? Explain.

   b) Show the symbolic steps to solve $n \div \frac{3}{4} = 6$.

10. Use the distributive property and the balancing method to find the value of x.

a)
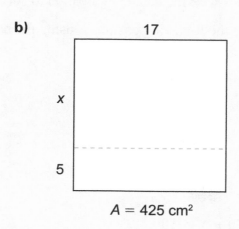

$A = 266 \text{ cm}^2$

b)

$A = 425 \text{ cm}^2$

11. Solve the following equations using the balancing method. Record your steps.

a) $-1\frac{1}{4}n = 20$

b) $-\frac{7}{10} + g = \frac{1}{3}$

c) $\frac{5}{m} = 20$

d) $k - 2 = -1$

12. a) Compare the following equations. Are any of these equivalent? Why?

$4x = 32$ $-4x = 32$ $4x = -32$ $-4x = -32$

b) Find the value of x that makes each equation true.

13. Each fall the seventh grade class at Woodrow Wilson Middle School sponsors a fund-raiser. For the fund-raiser, the students sell nutrition bars. They first have to buy the food they are selling. However, they sell each item for more than it costs and usually make a profit.

a) The students plan on selling nutrition bars for $3.00 each. They spent $55 to buy 100 bars. Write an expression for the profit made by selling n bars.

b) Write an equation that shows the number of bars they must sell in order to earn back their $55 investment. Solve your equation.

c) If the students sell all 100 bars, how much money will they raise?

14. In motocross racing, competitors race motorbikes on a dirt track. The handling of a motorbike is affected by the weight of the bike. Jared reduced the weight of his motorcycle by 9.6 pounds. It now weighs 121.8 pounds. Write an equation to show how much the motorbike weighed originally. Use m to represent the initial weight of the bike in pounds. Use the balancing method to solve for m.

15. Solve the following equations using the balancing method. Record your work.

    a) $-1 + x = 2$

    b) $-0.75x = 18$

    c) $x \div 4 = 23$

    d) $6 - x = 13$

    e) $x - 2\frac{3}{5} = 1\frac{3}{4}$

    f) $70 \div x = 10$

 Think Beyond

16. a) In one NASCAR race, Car 7 completed the $2\frac{1}{2}$-mile track in 1 minute. What was its speed in miles per hour?

    b) In the same race Car 12 completed one lap in 45 seconds. Was Car 12 traveling faster or slower than Car 7? What was Car 12's speed in miles per hour?

 **Think Beyond**

17. If two times a number is added to five times the number, the result is the sum of six times the number plus four. Find the number.

18. Name two numbers between $^-4.02$ and $^-4.03$.

19. True or False? If false, provide a counterexample.

    If a triangle has one acute angle, the other two angles cannot be acute.

20. Draw an equilateral triangle and shade in $\frac{2}{3}$. Write $\frac{2}{3}$ as a decimal and as a percent.

21. Spirit Day at the high school involves two events: College Dress Up and Wacky Hair. Students can participate in both, one or none of the events. In Homeroom 122, there are 24 students.

    Based on the diagram below, how many students in Homeroom 122 did not participate in either Spirit Day event?

    A. 2   **D.** 8

    B. 16   **E.** 6

    C. 14

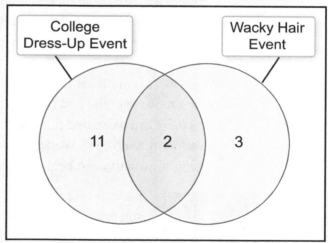

Homeroom 122 Spirit Day Participation

22. Louisa said that $^-\frac{5}{12} < ^-\frac{7}{12}$ because 5 is less than 7.

    Explain Louisa's mistake and correct it.

Solving More Equations

➡️ Start It Off

Look at the sequence from Lesson 2.3.

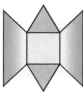

Stage 1   Stage 2   Stage 3

1. Use the table you built in the last lesson to find the explicit rule for this pattern. Use n to represent the stage number and T to represent the total number of blocks.

2. Using this explicit rule, what is the total number of blocks in the Stage 9? Stage 42? Stage 100?

3. We can show this sequence using a picture, a table and an algebraic rule. How are these representations related? Why would you want to show the same sequence in different ways?

You know two methods for solving equations. Now it is time to explore solving more complicated equations such as $3x - 2 = 10$ and $\frac{7+x}{2} = 8$. Since there are two operations in these equations, you must decide which operation to undo first. Working backwards through the order of operations or using flowcharts can help you solve these equations.

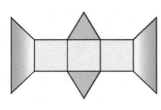

Waterskiing is a sport where you glide on top of the water as you are pulled by a boat. While most starting skiers use two skis, some advanced skiers use only one ski. Some people ski barefoot! There is a formula for barefoot skiers that relates the weight of the skier and speed of the boat. If you add 20 to one-tenth of a person's weight in pounds, you can find the speed of the boat for barefoot waterskiing.

Example 1

A given boat has a maximum speed of 35 mph. How large a barefoot skier (weight in pounds) can it pull? Let n represent the weight of the skier.

$\frac{n}{10} + 20 = 35$

One method for solving an equation like this one is to work backwards. A flowchart helps to solve the equation.

Flowchart

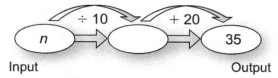

You can use undoing or the balancing method to determine the solution.

Solution Steps—Undoing

$\frac{n}{10} + 20 = 35$	Original equation
$\frac{n}{10} = 35 - 20$	Undo addition by subtracting 20.
$\frac{n}{10} = 15$	Simplify.
$n = 15 \cdot 10$	Undo division by multiplying by 10.
$n = 150$	Simplify.

The weight of the skier is 150 pounds.

$\frac{150}{10} \overset{?}{=} 15$	Check using substitution.
$15 = 15$	Correct

Solution Steps—Balancing

$\frac{n}{10} + 20 = 35$	Original equation
$\frac{n}{10} + 20 + {}^{-}20 = 35 + {}^{-}20$	Add the additive inverse of 20 to both sides.
$\frac{n}{10} = 15$	Simplify. $20 + {}^{-}20 = 0$
$10 \cdot \frac{n}{10} = 15 \cdot 10$	Multiply both sides by the multiplicative inverse of $\frac{1}{10}$.
$n = 150$	Simplify. $10 + \frac{1}{10} = 1$

The weight of the skier is 150 pounds.

$\frac{150}{10} \overset{?}{=} 15$	Check using substitution.
$15 = 15$	Correct

1. How are the two solution methods above the same? How are they different?

When solving equations that involve two or more operations, the hardest part is deciding which operation you should undo first. Three students were discussing the equation $5m - 3 = 27$.

2. a) Draw a flowchart to solve $5m - 3 = 27$.

   b) Show the steps to solve $5m - 3 = 27$. Check the solution.

3. a) Discuss with your partner how to solve the following equations. What do you do first? Sketch a flowchart to support your decision.

   i) $3c + 1 = 10$ ii) $\frac{1}{2}y - 4 = 14$ iii) $\frac{a - 9}{5} = 25$

   b) Solve each equation. Record the solution steps. Check your solutions.

4. a) What number can you multiply both sides of $^-x = {}^-4$ by in order to solve for x?

   b) Solve the equation $8 + {}^-m = 19$ for m. Check your solution.

5. a) Solve the equation $1 - 3m = 7$.

   b) Wayne changed the equation to an equivalent one, $1 + (^-3m) = 7$. Solve this equation.

   c) Which equation was easier to solve? Explain why.

Example 2

Karen signed up for three kneeboarding lessons. She also had to rent a kneeboard for $15 each time. If the total cost was $120, how much did each lesson cost? Let c represent the cost of each lesson.

This can be represented by using the equation: $3(c + 15) = 120$. Draw a flowchart to help you solve it.

Flowchart

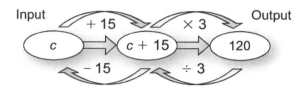

Examine the two methods for solving $3(c + 15) = 120$ for c.

Expand–First Solution Steps	**Multiply–First Solution Steps**
$3(c + 15) = 120$	$3(c + 15) = 120$
$3c + 45 = 120$	$\left(\frac{1}{3}\right)3(c + 15) = 120\left(\frac{1}{3}\right)$
$3c + 45 + {}^-45 = 120 + {}^-45$	$c + 15 = 40$
$3c = 75$	$c + 15 + {}^-15 = 40 + {}^-15$
$\left(\frac{1}{3}\right) \cdot (3c) = 75 \cdot \left(\frac{1}{3}\right)$	$c = 25$
$c = 25$	

Each lesson cost $25.

$$3(25 + 15) \stackrel{?}{=} 120$$
$$3(40) \stackrel{?}{=} 120 \qquad \text{Check by substitution}$$
$$120 = 120 \qquad \text{Correct}$$

6. Explain each step in the two solution methods above.

Wrap It Up

Understanding how to solve equations helps you apply algebra to the solution of problems. Explain how to solve $5(x - 3) = 25$ for x.

Write About It

Check all your solutions by substituting your answer into the original equation.

1. Give other middle school students some tips on how to solve equations that have two or more operations. Use examples.

2. Solve the following equations. Show all steps.

   a) $\dfrac{n+3}{8} = 1$

   b) $7n - 1 = -28$

   c) $12 - \dfrac{2}{3}m = 10$

   d) $7.5k = 42$

3. Write an equation that has a negative solution, and that can be solved using the balancing method by adding $-\dfrac{1}{2}$ to both sides.

    Hint
   See page 157

4. If 7 is subtracted from 8 times a number, the result is 9. Find the number.

5. Fill in the flowchart to represent the equation $-n + 9 = 36$. Show the steps to solve the equation.

   Input n 36   Output

6. Which equation does not require that you multiply both sides by a reciprocal to solve it?

   A. $7m = 144$

   B. $\dfrac{m}{6} = -18$

   C. $9 + n = 34$

   D. $-\dfrac{1}{2}n = 24$

7. Write an equation that has a non-integer solution and that can be solved using the balancing method by multiplying both sides by 4.

8. Solve the following equations.

   a) $n - 7\dfrac{5}{8} = 2\dfrac{11}{12}$

   b) $4(n + 2) = 6$

   c) $5 - 3n = 41$

   d) $2s - 6 = 8$

   e) $\dfrac{8}{9}x = \dfrac{12}{18}$

   f) $1.4 + b = 0.93$

   g) $\dfrac{3y}{8} = 9$

   h) $0 = \dfrac{m}{2} + 1$

   i) $6(y - 4) = 24$

9. A pharmacist found that she had filled $\frac{3}{4}$ of the prescriptions phoned in that morning. She filled 132 prescriptions. How many prescriptions were called in that morning?

10. Here is how Cornelia solved the equation $^-1 - k = 12$. Explain each of her steps.

? Hint
See page 157

$$^-1 - k = 12$$

$$1 + {}^-1 - k = 12 + 1$$

$$^-k = 13$$

$$(-1) \cdot {}^-k = 13 \cdot (-1)$$

$$k = {}^-13$$

11. Solve the following equations. Record your steps. It may help to draw flowcharts.

   a) $6 + 2n = 5$

   b) $16 = 4(k + 7)$

   c) $\frac{1 - m}{3} = 2$

   d) $\frac{n + 1}{3} = 5$

   e) $6 = 21 - (^-3n)$

   f) $-2(m - 5) = 20$

Think Back

12. Match the following.

a) {2, 3, 5, 7, 11, 13}   i) Factors of 16

b) {1, 2, 4, 5, 10, 20}   ii) Multiples of 2

c) {1, 4, 9, 16, 25}   iii) Square numbers

d) {2, 4, 6, 8, 16}   iv) Prime numbers

e) {1, 2, 4, 8, 16}   v) Factors of 20

13. Two cards have numbers on the front and back. The fronts of the cards are shown below.

When you add the front or back of the first card to the front or back of the second card you get one of the following sums: 14, 16, 17, 19.

What numbers are on the back of each card?

14. Show all steps to evaluate $0.3412 \div 0.04$.

15. Hot dogs are sold in packages of 12. Hot dog buns are sold in packages of 8. What is the least number of packages of hot dogs and buns you need to buy to have exactly one hot dog bun for every hot dog?

16. Find the average of 23, 18, 13, ⁻4 and ⁻8.

Optional Technology Lesson for this section available in your eBook

Sum It Up

When you solve an equation with one variable, you find the specific value or values of the variable that make the equation true. In this unit, you learned two methods to solve equations.

Solving Equations by the Undoing Method

Flowcharts are useful tools to evaluate an expression or to solve an equation. Follow the direction of the arrows to perform the calculations shown in the flowchart. For example, $4 \cdot 2 + 3$ is shown as:

You can also work backwards through a flowchart by undoing each operation.

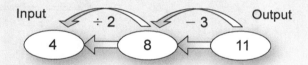

You can use inverse operations to undo expressions and solve equations.

- $y + 7 = 13$ The inverse operation of addition is subtraction. $y = 13 - 7$
- $x - (^-2) = 10$ The inverse operation of subtraction is addition. $x = 10 + (^-2)$
- $4p = 18$ The inverse operation of multiplication is division. $p = 18 \div 4$
- $\frac{x}{9} = ^-8$ The inverse operation of division is multiplication. $x = ^-8 \cdot 9$

Solving Equations by the Balancing Method

You can solve equations by using additive and multiplicative inverses and properties of equality. Balance scales illustrate this method.

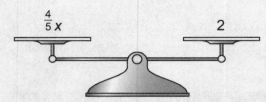

Example 1

$$\frac{4}{5}x = 2$$

$$\left(\frac{5}{4}\right)\frac{4}{5}x = 2\left(\frac{5}{4}\right)$$ Balance the equation by multiplying both sides by the reciprocal of $\frac{4}{5}$.

$$x = \frac{10}{4} = 2\frac{1}{2}$$ Simplify

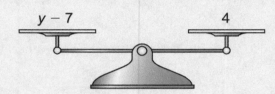

Example 2

$$y - 7 = 4$$

$$y + {}^{-}7 = 4$$ Rewrite the subtraction equation as an equivalent addition equation.

$$y + {}^{-}7 + 7 = 4 + 7$$ Balance the equation by adding the additive inverse of $^{-}7$ to both sides of the equal sign.

$$y = 11$$

Solving More Complex Equations

To find the value of m in $^-3m + 27 = 39$, you can use the undoing method or the balancing method. It may help to put the equation into a flowchart.

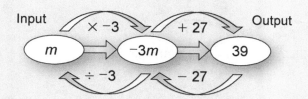

Use the undoing method to work backward through the equation using inverse operations.

$$^-3m + 27 = 39$$

$$^-3m = 39 + ^-27 \qquad \text{Undo the addition by subtraction.}$$

$$^-3m = 12$$

$$m = \frac{12}{^-3} \qquad \text{Undo the multiplication by division.}$$

$$m = ^-4$$

Use the balancing method and perform the same operations on both sides of the equal sign.

$$^-3m + 27 = 39$$

$$^-3m + 27 + ^-27 = 39 + ^-27 \qquad \text{Add the additive inverse, } ^-27, \text{ to both sides.}$$

$$^-3m = 12 \qquad\qquad\qquad 27 + ^-27 = 0.$$

$$^-\tfrac{1}{3} \cdot ^-3m = 12 \cdot ^-\tfrac{1}{3} \qquad \text{Multiply both sides by the multiplicative inverse, } ^-\tfrac{1}{3}.$$

$$m = ^-4 \qquad\qquad\qquad ^-3 \cdot ^-\tfrac{1}{3} = 1.$$

MATHEMATICALLY SPEAKING

Do you know what these mathematical terms mean?

▶ addition property of equality   ▶ flowchart   ▶ multiplication property of equality

▶ explicit rule   ▶ inverse operations   ▶ recursive (iterative) rule

Study Guide

Solving Equations

Part 1. What did you learn?

1. Alessio, Brett and Camden are brothers. Brett is 16 years old. Alessio used the flowchart below to show how his age compared to his brother's age.

a. What is Alessio's age?

b. Alessio said the expression $\frac{1}{2}c + 3$ is equal to his age, where the letter c represents Camden's age in years. How old is Camden?

2. Match each equation in Column A with the equation in Column B that could be used to "undo" the operation to solve the equation. Then, find the solution to the equation in Column C.

Column A	Column B	Column C
(a) $-50x = -100$	(f) $x = \frac{20}{40}$	(k) $x = 2$
(b) $x + 2\frac{1}{3} = \frac{1}{3}$	(g) $x = -1 + {}^-7$	(l) $x = 8$
(c) $x - (-7) = -1$	(h) $x = 6 \cdot \frac{4}{3}$	(m) $x = 0.5$
(d) $\frac{3}{4}x = 6$	(i) $x = \frac{1}{3} - 2\frac{1}{3}$	(n) $x = -8$
(e) $40x = 20$	(j) $x = \frac{-100}{-50}$	(o) $x = -2$

3. Explain each step in the solution below.

Step	Explanation
(a) $2n - 4.5 = 16.5$	Original equation
(b) $2n + {}^-4.5 = 16.5$	
(c) $2n + {}^-4.5 + 4.5 = 16.5 + 4.5$	
(d) $\frac{1}{2} \cdot 2n = 21 \cdot \frac{1}{2}$	
(e) $n = 10.5$	

4. Use the explanation given to record the steps in the solution below.

Step	Explanation
(a) $6 - \frac{3}{4}x = ^-6$	Original equation
(b)	Rewrite subtraction as addition of the opposite.
(c)	Undo add 6 by adding $^-6$ to both sides.
(d)	Undo multiplying by $-\frac{3}{4}$ by multiplying by its multiplicative inverse, $-\frac{4}{3}$.
(e)	Write the solution.

5. Solve each of the equations below. Show your steps.

   a. $x - 12 = 14.5$

   b. $\frac{2}{3}n = 6$

   c. $\frac{3}{4}m + 4 = 19$

   d. $6 - 2p = ^-8$

6. Use substitution to check to see if each of your solutions from Question 5 is correct. Show your work.

7. Write an equation that requires the use of the addition property of equality where $^-2.5$ must be added to both sides of the equation and the solution is not an integer.

8. Write an equation that requires the use of the multiplication property of equality where both sides of the equation are multiplied by $\frac{3}{2}$ and the solution is an integer.

9. Write and solve an equation that could be solved by adding $^-2$ to both sides and then multiplying both sides by $^-1$. Show and explain each step.

10. Pierro is training to run a half-marathon. He ran 11 miles on Tuesday. This was 2 more than three times the number of miles he ran on Monday. Write and solve an equation to determine the number of miles Pierro ran on Monday. Show your steps.

11. Isabel and Rocco worked individually to solve the equation $\frac{x}{3} + 4 = -3$. When they had each found a solution, they exchanged papers and found that they used very different steps. Here is a copy of each student's explanation.

Isabel's explanation	Rocco's explanation
Balance by subtracting 4 from both sides.	Undo add 4 by adding -4 to both sides.
Maintain balance by multiplying both sides by 3.	Undo multiplying by $\frac{1}{3}$ by multiplying both sides by the reciprocal, 3.
Write the solution.	Write the solution.

a. Follow Isabel's explanation and write the steps that she used.

b. Follow Rocco's explanation and write the steps that he used.

c. Did both explanations lead to the same, correct solution? Why or why not?

12. Beth-Anne's older sister Ruthie told her that she can solve any two-step equation using only addition and multiplication. Beth-Anne said, "Prove it!" She asked Ruthie to solve $4 + 6n = 1$ using only addition and multiplication. Can this be done? Why or why not?

13. Ollie used inverse operations to solve $x - 4 = 12$. Here is what he did:

$$x - 4 = 12$$
$$x + 4 - 4 = 12 - 4$$
$$x = 8$$

What error(s) did Ollie make? What would you say or do to help Ollie realize and fix his error(s)?

14. Adrienne solved the equation $45 - d = 60$. Here is what she did:

$$45 - d = 60$$
$$45 - d - 45 = 60 - 45$$
$$d = 15$$

What error(s) did Adrienne make? What would you say or do to help Adrienne find and fix her error(s)?

15. Ala was asked the following multiple-choice question on a recent quiz:

Piper's new car gets 30 miles to the gallon. Her car's gas tank holds 20 gallons of gas. Which equation could be used to find m, the number of miles Piper can travel on one tank of gas?

A. $30(20) = m$ **C.** $30 + 20 = m$

B. $20m = 30$ **D.** $30m = 20$

Ala chose Answer D because she thinks that "$30m$" stands for 30 miles. What is wrong with Ala's reasoning? Which is the correct answer? Why?

SECTION 3

Representing Linear Patterns Using Equations, Graphs and Tables

Mathematical patterns are all around us. Baseball players use patterns to run to the right location to catch a fly ball. Golfers use patterns to predict where the ball will land after they "tee off." Many teams have patterns on their jerseys. In this section, you will explore linear, or straight-line, patterns.

Linear patterns are based on a particular type of relationship and can be shown using graphs, tables, words and equations. Algebraic expressions and equations with variables are particularly useful in describing linear situations and relationships.

LESSON 3.1 Linear Patterns

Start It Off

Wilson, a seventh grader, sold bottles of water to observers during a road race. The table shows the number of bottles Wilson sold during each hour.

Time	Bottles Sold
11 am	30
Noon	35
1 pm	43
2 pm	40
3 pm	25
4 pm	23
5 pm	10
6 pm	8
7 pm	4

1. Make a coordinate graph of the data in the table. Label the axes and give the graph a title.

2. How did you determine the scale for each axis?

3. Should you connect the points on the graph? Why or why not?

4. What does the graph tell you about the race?

Marathons are road races that are approximately 26 miles long (26 miles 385 yards to be exact). Over 450,000 people in the United States participate in marathons each year.

Linear Relationships

How long does it take to run a marathon? Today, technology is used to measure time. Runners are given "timing chips" to tie onto their sneakers. These chips send a radio signal each time runners pass over a pad along the course. Friends and relatives can receive updates on the pacing of a runner via computers, cell phones or other devices.

Lyman and Catherine are serious athletes who train for marathons. One year they ran the Walt Disney World® Marathon, which goes through the Magic Kingdom®, Epcot® and Disney's Hollywood Studios™. One thing that makes this marathon fun is that you run through Cinderella's Castle and then receive a quick hug from Winnie the Pooh on the other side!

Lyman and Catherine each kept a steady pace throughout the race by monitoring their own progress on GPS devices. Their times are shown in the following tables.

Lyman's Progress	
Time (hr.)	Distance (mi.)
0	0
$\frac{1}{4}$	$2\frac{1}{2}$
$\frac{1}{2}$	5
$\frac{3}{4}$	$7\frac{1}{2}$
1	10
$1\frac{1}{4}$	$12\frac{1}{2}$
$1\frac{1}{2}$	15
$1\frac{3}{4}$	$17\frac{1}{2}$
2	20
$2\frac{1}{4}$	$22\frac{1}{2}$
$2\frac{1}{2}$	25

Catherine's Progress	
Time (hr.)	Distance (mi.)
0	0
$\frac{1}{4}$	2
$\frac{1}{2}$	4
$\frac{3}{4}$	6
1	8
$1\frac{1}{4}$	10
$1\frac{1}{2}$	12
$1\frac{3}{4}$	14
2	16
$2\frac{1}{4}$	18
$2\frac{1}{2}$	20
$2\frac{3}{4}$	22
3	24
$3\frac{1}{4}$	26

1. Make a coordinate graph of the time and distance data in Lyman's table. Show time on the *x*-axis.

2. Use your graph to answer the following:

   a) Identify the variables on the graph.

   b) Describe the pattern created by graphing the points from the table.

   c) Does it make sense to connect the points with a line? Explain. If it does make sense, do it.

   d) Does it make sense to extend the line beyond the points given? Why or why not?

3. Continue to examine the graph of Lyman's marathon race.

   a) What do the coordinates $(1\frac{1}{2}, 15)$ represent?

   b) Marathons are just a bit longer than 26 miles. Explain how to use the graph to estimate the time it took Lyman to finish the marathon.

Some relationships between variables have special names. The graph of a linear relationship is a straight line.

MATHEMATICALLY SPEAKING

▶ linear relationship

Compare your graph to the one below. The coordinate pairs represent how many miles Lyman has run in a given number of hours (time, distance). The graph shows a linear relationship between distance and time during Lyman's marathon race.

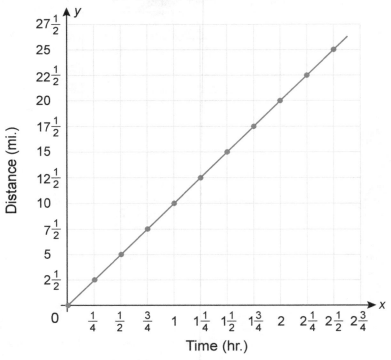

Lyman's Running Progress in the Walt Disney World® Marathon

Linear relationships can also be identified by recursive rules.

 **Let's Review**

A recursive rule is one that enables you to find a new value by using a previous result. The next value in the sequence shown in this table is determined using the rule: *new = previous + 6*. In this case, it is 36 (*new = 30 + 6*). Note that the stage numbers are sequential integers: 1, 2, 3, ...

Stage Number	Value
0	0
1	6
2	12
3	18
4	24
5	30
6	?

Examine the relationships between time and distance in the tables below. Lyman's distance increased by 2.5 miles for each $\frac{1}{4}$ hour he ran, 5 miles for each $\frac{1}{2}$ hour, and 10 miles for each hour.

Time (hr.)	Term Number (number of $\frac{1}{4}$ hours)	Distance (mi.)
0	0	0
$\frac{1}{4}$	1	$2\frac{1}{2}$
$\frac{1}{2}$	2	5
$\frac{3}{4}$	3	$7\frac{1}{2}$
1	4	10
$1\frac{1}{4}$	5	$12\frac{1}{2}$
$1\frac{1}{2}$	6	15
$1\frac{3}{4}$	7	$17\frac{1}{2}$
2	8	20
$2\frac{1}{4}$	9	$22\frac{1}{2}$
$2\frac{1}{2}$	10	25

Time (hr.)	Term Number (number of $\frac{1}{2}$ hours)	Distance (mi.)
0	0	0
$\frac{1}{2}$	1	5
1	2	10
$1\frac{1}{2}$	3	15
2	4	20
$2\frac{1}{2}$	5	25

Time (hr.)	Term Number (number of 1 hours)	Distance (mi.)
0	0	0
1	1	10
2	2	20

The three recursive rules shown in the tables represent the same situation. For each $\frac{1}{4}$–hour increment, the new distance is the previous distance plus 2.5 miles. For each $\frac{1}{2}$–hour increment, the new distance is the previous distance plus 5 miles. For each 1–hour increment, the new distance is the previous distance plus 10 miles.

In a linear relationship, the variables stand for quantities that change at the same rate in relationship to each other. You can identify a linear relationship by its graph by noticing that all of the points form a straight line. You can identify a linear relationship by its recursive rule by noting that a constant value is repeatedly added or subtracted as you move from one value to the next: *new = previous + constant*.

4. Examine the table of Catherine's marathon progress. Do you think the relationship between Catherine's times and distances is linear? Using a different color, plot Catherine's data points on the same graph with Lyman's and connect the points.

5. Is there a recursive rule relating Catherine's distances? If so, write the recursive rule for determining Catherine's distance for every $\frac{1}{2}$ hour of running.

6. Compare the lines that represent Lyman's and Catherine's running pace. Who is the faster runner? Explain how you can tell who the faster runner is by using the graph, by using the table, and by using the recursive rules.

7. Even though the graph and the data from the table indicate that Lyman kept a very steady pace of 5 miles per every half hour, do you think that in reality he kept a steady pace per minute? Why or why not?

In mathematics, we talk of speed as a distance traveled in a given time period, such as 10 miles in 1 hour. This is actually the average speed, which is a ratio of the distance traveled over the time elapsed $\left(\frac{10 \text{ miles}}{1 \text{ hour}}\right.$, or 10 miles per hour$\left.\right)$. We also call this average speed the rate.

Nonlinear Relationships

Elizabeth, a friend of Catherine and Lyman's, is not a runner. "I'll run a marathon when 'pigs fly,'" she declared. "Wonderful," replied Lyman. "I'll enter you into the Flying Pig Marathon in Cincinnati ."

The Flying Pig Marathon is the country's third most popular marathon for first-timers. The marathon adheres to the "flying pig" theme down to almost every detail, with costumed runners, volunteers known as "grunts," "squealing fans" lining the sidelines, and an official race mascot greeting runners at the "finish swine." With some coaxing, Elizabeth attempted the Flying Pig Marathon. Her progress in the race is displayed in the table below.

Elizabeth's Progress	
Time (hr.)	Distance (mi.)
0	0
$\frac{1}{4}$	2
$\frac{1}{2}$	3
$\frac{3}{4}$	4
1	5
$1\frac{1}{4}$	5
$1\frac{1}{2}$	6
$1\frac{3}{4}$	6
2	8
$2\frac{1}{4}$	9
$2\frac{1}{2}$	10
$2\frac{3}{4}$	10
3	10

8. Make a coordinate graph of the time and distance data in Elizabeth's table. Display time on the *x*-axis and use the same scales as before.

9. **a)** Describe the graphical pattern of Elizabeth's data. Is the relationship between time and distance linear? Why or why not?

   b) Imagine that you are a Flying Pig commentator. Write a news report on Elizabeth's progress. Mention her average speed along different parts of the course and explain what she was doing at different times.

10. Examine Elizabeth's data table. Can you find a recursive relationship describing her progress? What do your results tell you about the type of relationship that exists between Elizabeth's time and distance?

Some relationships between two variables do not produce straight-line graphs. These relationships are known as nonlinear relationships. Some nonlinear graphs look like curves. Others have segments that are straight but the overall graph is not a straight line. In a nonlinear relationship, the recursive rule does *not* involve adding or subtracting the same constant amount. In fact, there may not be a recursive rule that describes the relationship of one term to the next. The graphs below are examples of nonlinear relationships.

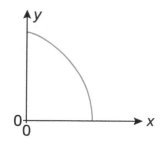 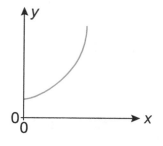 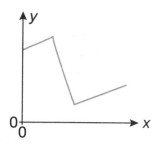 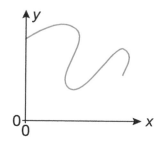

Wrap It Up

What are the differences between linear relationships and nonlinear relationships? Explain the characteristics of these types of relationships as seen in graphs, tables and recursive rules.

Write
About It

1. Imagine you are running the Flying Pig Marathon. Create a table of time/distance data and its corresponding graph. Is the relationship between time and distance linear? Explain how this is shown in the table and in the graph.

2. Regular gasoline is selling for $2.39 per gallon, while the price for premium gasoline is $2.59 per gallon.

   a) Make two tables that show the cost of various numbers of gallons of each grade of gasoline. Define your variables.

   b) Graph the cost of purchasing regular gasoline and the cost of purchasing premium gasoline on the same coordinate grid. Use the x-axis for number of gallons.

   c) Are the relationships between the number of gallons of each gasoline purchased and the cost linear? Explain.

3. Here is a graph of the cost of CDs. Does it make sense to connect the points on the graph? Why or why not?

   ? Hint
   See page 157

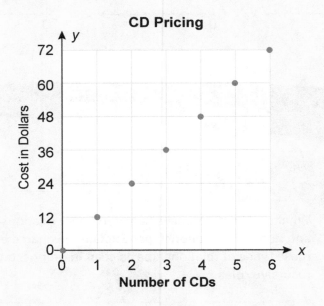

4. Examine the following graphs. Discuss the relationship between time and population in each graph. Which graphs appear to be linear?

a)
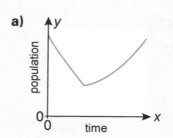

b)
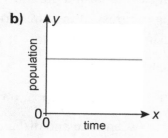

c)
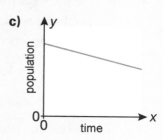

d)
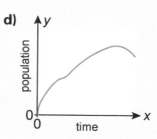

Most people do not run marathons, but many people walk to get exercise. Examine the tables that show the number of meters walked by three friends. Use the tables for Questions 5–8.

Crystal	
Time (sec.)	Distance (m)
0	0
1	2
2	4
3	6
4	8
5	10
6	12
7	14

Leroy	
Time (sec.)	Distance (m)
0	0
2	5
4	10
6	15
8	20
10	25
12	30
14	35

Chris	
Time (sec.)	Distance (m)
0	0
1	1
2	2
3	3
4	4
5	5
6	6
7	7

5. a) Which of the three friends walks the fastest? How can you tell?

 **Hint**
See page 157

b) If Leroy continues walking at this pace, what is his average walking rate per minute?

c) If Chris improved his speed and was able to walk 6 meters in 1 second, how far would he walk in 1 minute? In 1 hour?

6. a) Copy and extend Crystal's and Chris' tables to show the distance walked by each student for the first 12 seconds assuming they walk at a steady pace. What patterns do you notice?

b) Write a rule for each table that describes the distance walked in the first t seconds.

7. **a)** Use the data from each table and plot the (time, distance) points. Graph the walking progress of the three friends on the same coordinate grid using a different color for each.

   b) What are the variables?

   c) How does a faster walking pace appear on the graph?

8. Are the relationships between time and distance walked by Crystal, Leroy and Chris linear? How can you tell?

9. Write recursive rules for the output values in the following tables.

   a)

Term Number	Output
0	0
1	13
2	26
3	39
4	52
5	

   b)

Term Number	Output
0	2
1	5
2	8
3	11
4	14
5	

   c) Copy and extend both tables to the 8th term. Fill in the outputs.

   d) Graph the data from Part b.

10. **a)** The cost of buying current songs at one Web-based store is $1.29. Build a table of values to show how much it will cost to buy up to eight songs. Label each column of your table using a variable.

   b) What do the variables in your table represent?

   c) Write a recursive rule for buying songs at this Web-based store.

   d) Imagine graphing the points in your table. Should they be connected? Why or why not?

   e) Is this a linear relationship? Explain.

11. Claire simplified the expression $-8(2 - 6k)$ and chose answer D below as her solution. Did Claire make the right choice? If so, explain why. If not, what did Claire do wrong and what is the correct option?

    A. $-16 + 48k$

    B. $-16 - 6k$

    C. $-16 - 48k$

    D. $-16 + 6k$

12. Write "28 strawberries in 16 ounces of fruit salad" as a unit rate.

13. Make a list of three geometric solids that roll.

14. Which of the following measurement units is most appropriate for measuring the distance from your hometown to the equator? Explain your choice.

    A. millimeter

    B. centimeter

    C. meter

    D. kilometer

15. Solve $112 = -4c + 84$. Show your work.

Increasing and Decreasing Relationships

 Start It Off

Table A	
x	y
−8	−16
−6	−12
−2	−4
0	0
5	10
10	20

Table B	
x	y
−10	20
−7	14
0	0
2	−4
4	−8
9	−18

1. Plot the points from the two tables on one graph. Connect the points from each table and extend them using a ruler. Label the lines A and B.

2. Compare the graphs of A and B. How are they similar and how are they different?

3. For each table, write an explicit rule for finding the value of y for any value of x.

4. Do the variables, x and y stand for specific unknowns, related varying quantities, or many unrelated values?

Have you ever watched an auto race? If so, it was probably organized by the National Association for Stock Car Auto Racing (NASCAR). NASCAR races have grown to become the second most popular professional sporting events in terms of television ratings in the United States.

NASCAR races are held on many different tracks that vary in length and design. One of the best-known tracks is the 2.5-mile long Daytona International Speedway.

1. The Daytona 500 race is 500 miles long. How many laps must a racecar make to complete the race? Note: A lap is one complete trip around the track.

2. **a)** If the average speed of Car 8 is 160 mph, approximately how long will it take the racer to complete the Daytona 500? Give your response in hours and minutes.

   b) At the average speed of 160 mph, approximately how many minutes will it take Car 8 to make one lap around the track? Approximately how many seconds? Use a ratio table like the one below.

Miles	160	80	40				
Minutes	60	30	15				

Increasing Linear Relationships

MATHEMATICALLY SPEAKING

▶ increasing linear relationship

The graph below records another car's performance in the Daytona 500. Notice that as time, t, increases, the total distance, D, increases. We see that this relationship is linear because it is represented by a straight line. As the x-values increase by a set amount, so do the y-values. Since both variables are increasing at the same time, we say that it is an increasing linear relationship. Graphs of increasing linear relationships are lines that go up from left to right.

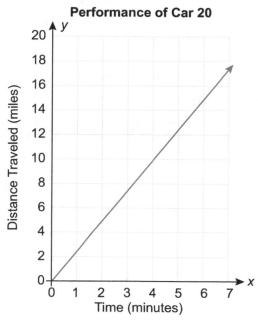

Performance of Car 20

3. a) What is Car 20's speed in miles per minute? At this rate, how far will Car 20 travel in 8 minutes? 10 minutes?

b) Use the graph to describe in words the relationship between time and distance for Car 20. Incorporate the word *increasing* into your description.

c) Determine a recursive rule for finding the total distance for the next minute of time using *previous* and *new*. Explain how your recursive rule shows that this is an increasing linear relationship.

A recursive rule is not especially useful if you want to find the distance traveled after 45 minutes or after 2 hours (120 minutes) of Car 20. It is easier to use an explicit rule. With an explicit rule you can find the distance traveled at any desired time during the race.

 **Let's Review** An explicit rule is an equation that directly defines the y variable, or output variable, in terms of the x variable, or input variable.

Below are the time/distance data for Car 20. Notice that as the time increases by 1 minute, the distance increases by 2.5 miles.

t	D
Time (min.)	Total Distance (miles)
0	0
1	2.5
2	5.0
3	7.5
4	10.0
5	12.5
6	15.0
n	

4. Using the data in the table above:

   a) Find the explicit rule that relates the total distance, D, and the time, t, in minutes.

   b) The formula $D = rt$ can help us make sense of this situation. What does r represent?

   c) Use your explicit rule to find the distance covered in 2 hours 13 minutes.

   d) Determine how long it would take Car 20 to complete the Daytona 500.

   e) What is the average speed of Car 20 in miles per hour?

At some NASCAR events, banners made up of geometric designs and flags line the racetrack.

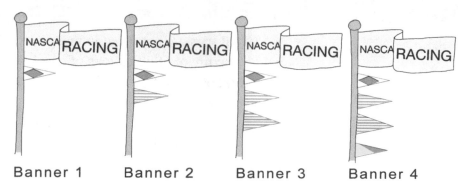

Banner 1   Banner 2   Banner 3   Banner 4

Listing the information in an expanded table can help you describe the pattern in the flags shown above with variables. Look for a part of the pattern that stays the same each time. Recall that we refer to this value as a *constant*, because it doesn't change from term to term. In the banners, the big rectangular NASCAR flag and the post don't change; they are the constant features. The feature that changes or varies each time is the number of small flags on the post.

5. **a)** What patterns do you notice in the banners?

   b) Copy and complete the table below. Note that each term has one more flag than the previous term.

Term Number (position of banners)	Total Number of Objects Needed to Make a Banner	Constant + Variation (big flag and post + little flags)
1	3	2 + 1
2	4	2 + 2
3	5	2 + 3
4		
5		
24		
n		

6. a) What is meant by the "n^{th}" banner?

    b) Use the expanded table to determine the explicit rule for the number of objects needed to make a banner.

    c) Use your rule to verify how many objects are needed to make the 35th banner in the sequence.

    d) What number banner in the sequence is made up of 17 different objects?

Decreasing Linear Relationships

NASCAR cars are regulated in many ways. For example, the fuel tanks can hold a maximum of 22 gallons of gasoline. One car in the Indianapolis (or Indy) 500 has a fuel efficiency of 4.5 miles per gallon. Examine the graph below.

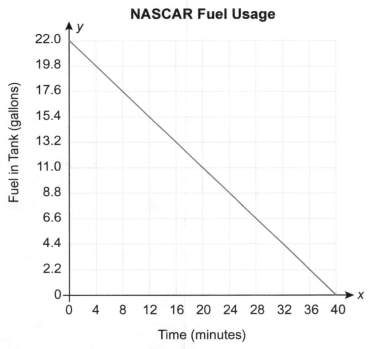

NASCAR Fuel Usage

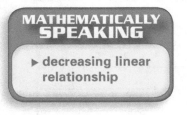

MATHEMATICALLY
SPEAKING

▶ decreasing linear
   relationship

7. Make a table of values for this graph. Remember that the x-value is usually the input and the y-value is the output.

Some linear relationships are classified as decreasing. In decreasing linear relationships, the output decreases as the input increases. The recursive rule for a decreasing linear relationship involves adding a negative constant to the previous value (*new = previous + constant*). The graph of a decreasing linear relationship is a line slanted downward from left to right.

8. **a)** Use the graph and/or the table to determine the recursive rule for how the amount of fuel in the tank changes each minute.

   b) Your rule will only be valid for times between 0 and 40 minutes. Why?

9. **a)** How many gallons of gasoline are used every minute?

   b) How do you determine the number of gallons left after a set number of minutes?

   c) Write an explicit rule for this situation.

10. Give two reasons why the relationship between time and gallons of gasoline used is linear. How can you determine that it is decreasing?

11. **a)** How far can this NASCAR car travel on one tank?

   b) How often will it have to refuel during the Indianapolis 500?

   c) What is the average speed of this car?

Wrap It Up

One method of paying for highway tolls is to put money into an account each month and have the toll amount removed electronically each time you drive through the tollbooth. Is the relationship between amount in the account, *c*, per month and the number of tolls, *n*, an increasing or decreasing relationship? Is it linear? Explain why or why not.

MATHEMATICALLY SPEAKING

▸ decreasing linear relationship

▸ increasing linear relationship

Write About It

1. When you examine a table or a graph, describe how you tell if the relationship between the two variables is increasing or decreasing. How do you tell if the relationship is linear?

2. Match each situation with its graph.

   a) The tea cooled off as time passed.

   b) The temperature in the valley rose steadily during the morning hours.

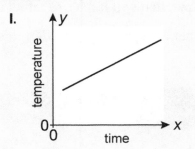

3. The Phoenix International Raceway recently hosted a 312-mile race. The data for Car 29 in the race are given, and they are linear.

Time (min.)	Total Distance (miles)
0	0
$\frac{1}{2}$	1.1
1	2.2
$1\frac{1}{2}$	3.3
2	4.4
$2\frac{1}{2}$	5.5
n	

   a) Explain how you can verify that the relationship between time and distance is linear.

   b) Determine a recursive rule that describes this relationship.

   Hint
   See page 158

c) Find the explicit rule that relates total distance and time. Check that your rule works for values in the table.

d) Using your rule, predict how long it will take Car 29 to complete the race.

e) Is this a realistic prediction? Why or why not?

4. During a recent running of the Daytona 500, Car 19 completed one lap of the track in 54 seconds. Recall that the track is 2.5 miles long.

a) In what fraction of a minute did Car 19 complete one lap? Record this as a simplified fraction and as a decimal.

b) How fast, in miles per hour, was Car 19 traveling during the lap?

5. After a skydiver jumps out of an airplane, she free-falls for a short period of time before releasing her parachute. As she falls, she picks up speed because of the force of gravity. The graph below shows the free-fall period of time.

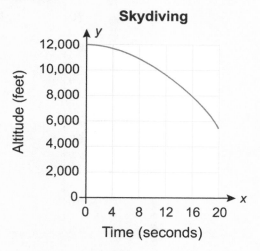

a) Describe the variables in the graph.

b) Is the relationship between these variables linear or nonlinear? How can you tell?

c) Is the relationship between the variables increasing or decreasing? How can you tell?

d) What was the height of the skydiver when she jumped?

e) How does the speed of the skydiver change over time? Why?

6. The number of minutes that a scuba diver can be underwater is related to his depth. Examine the table and graph.

Depth (feet)	Time Underwater (minutes)
50	80
60	55
70	45
80	35
90	25
100	22
110	15
120	12

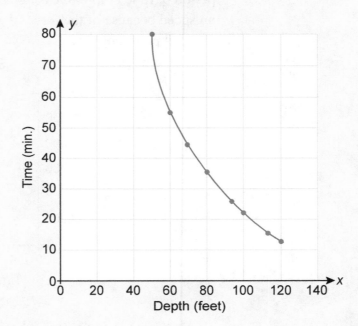

a) Is the relationship between time and depth linear or nonlinear? How can you tell?

b) Is the relationship increasing or decreasing? Explain.

7. Sound travels about 1 mile in 5 seconds, but light travels 1 mile almost instantly. Because sound travels much more slowly than light, you see lightning from a distant storm before you hear a thunder clap. There is a relationship between the time between a flash of lightning and a thunder clap, *t*, and your distance from the storm, *d*.

a) If you hear thunder and see lightning at the same time, what does this tell you about the location of the storm?

b) Complete the table below.

Time Between Lightning and Thunder t (seconds)	0	5	10	15	20	25
Distance from Storm d (miles)						

c) Write an explicit rule to represent the relationship between the distance, *d*, from a storm and the time, *t*, between seeing and hearing it.

8. Classify the following tables and graphs as linear increasing, linear decreasing or nonlinear.

a)

x	y
0	25
1	25
2	12
3	13
4	15
5	7

b)

x	y
0	0
1	3
2	6
3	9
4	12
5	15

c)

x	y
0	80
1	75
2	70
3	65
4	60
5	55

d)

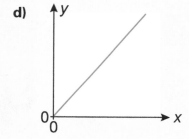

e)

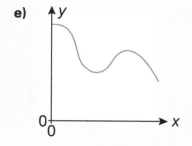

f)

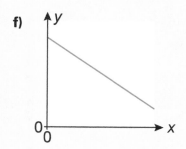

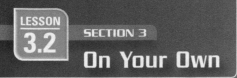
In 9–11, sketch a graph of the relationship. Assume it is linear. Identify the variables.

9. During a sale on plasma TVs, the number of TVs in the warehouse declined as the number of sales in the store increased.

10. The total cost for turkey sandwiches increased as the number of people at the meeting ordering a turkey sandwich increased.

11. The cost of a museum ticket is the same for people of all ages.

Think Back

12. Estimate the difference: $\frac{11}{15} - \frac{1}{3}$. Then, find the exact difference.

13. If the area of a triangle is 24 square meters, what are the possible whole number lengths of the base and height?

14. Write this statement as an equation: Two times the difference of d and ten is twenty-six. Solve the equation.

15. Determine the quotient of $0.85 \div 0.2$. Show your work.

16. Describe the mistakes made in solving this equation.

$$3y - 9 = 24$$
$$-6y = 24$$
$$\left(\frac{1}{6}\right) - 6y = 24\left(\frac{1}{6}\right)$$
$$y = -4$$

LESSON 3.3 Explicit Rules

Start It Off

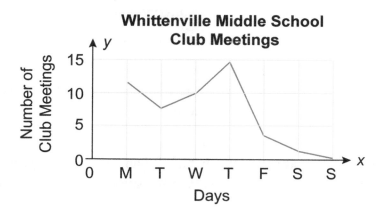

Whittenville Middle School Club Meetings

Number of Club Meetings (y-axis): 0, 5, 10, 15
Days (x-axis): M T W T F S S

1. Describe what this graph tells you about Whittenville Middle School. What doesn't this graph tell you about Whittenville's clubs?

2. Find a mistake in the graph.

3. What is the average number of daily club meetings at Whittenville Middle School in a week?

Linking Drawings, Tables and Rules

A fence is being built around a local soccer field. The fence consists of vertical posts every 8 feet with two horizontal rails between posts. There is a definite pattern to the construction of the fence.

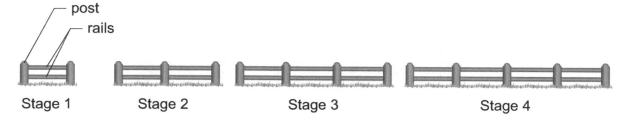

post — rails

Stage 1   Stage 2   Stage 3   Stage 4

1. Draw a picture of Stages 5 and 6 of the fence construction.

2. In a sentence or two, describe what Stage 10 of the fence will look like.

3. Make a table for the fence pattern data, showing the first ten stage numbers and the total number of pieces of fencing (posts and rails) needed.

4. a) Describe in words the recursive rule for this pattern. Use the words *previous* and *new* in your rule.

   b) What strategy might you use to find Stage 150 of the fence?

There are strategies you can use to help you determine the explicit rule for a set of data. One strategy is to *expand* the table and record observable growth patterns.

Example 1

One student, Cassandra, noticed that a left-hand post is always connected to two rails, leaving one end-post on the right. She marked this pattern of three pieces of wood on the first few stages.

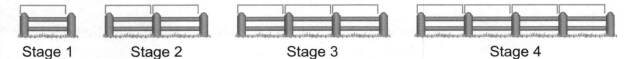

Stage 1   Stage 2   Stage 3   Stage 4

Cassandra called these three pieces the "fencing" and the one extra post, the "end-post." She added another column to her table to show this pattern.

Cassandra's Expanded Table		
Stage Number (*n*)	Total Number of Rails and Posts (*T*)	Pieces of Fencing + End-Post
1	4	3 + 1 = (3 • 1) + 1
2	7	6 + 1 = (3 • 2) + 1
3	10	9 + 1 = (3 • 3) + 1
4	13	12 + 1
5	16	15 + 1
6	19	18 + 1
7		
8		
n		

5. a) Look at the far right column of the table. Explain what $9 + 1$ in Stage 3 represents.

    b) Copy and complete the table for Stages 7 and 8.

    c) In each expression in the far right column, represent the number of pieces of fencing as a multiple of 3. For example, $9 + 1 = (3 \cdot 3) + 1$. What patterns do you notice?

    d) Write an explicit rule that relates the stage number, n, and the total number of pieces of fencing needed, T. Check that your rule works for all stages.

Example 2

Another student, Wayne, noticed a different fence pattern. He circled sets of rails.

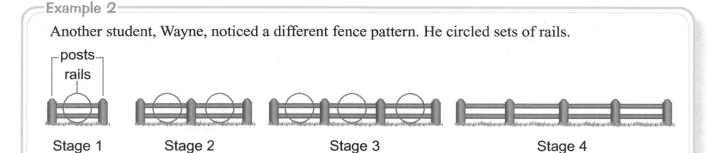

Stage 1   Stage 2   Stage 3   Stage 4

In each stage there are a set number of vertical posts and horizontal rails. He filled in the far right column of his table to show the number of posts and the number of rails for each stage.

Wayne's Expanded Table		
Stage Number (*n*)	Total Number of Rails and Posts (*T*)	Posts + Rails
1	4	$2 + 2 = 2 + (2 \cdot 1)$
2	7	$3 + 4 = 3 + (2 \cdot 2)$
3	10	$4 + 6$
4	13	$5 + 8$
5	16	$6 + 10$
6	19	$7 + 12$
7		
8		
n		

---

6. a) Describe in words how the number of posts and the number of rails are changing with the stage number.

    b) Copy the table and fill the number of posts and rails for the Stages 7 and 8. For all stages, represent the number of rails in each expression as a multiple of 2 in the third column.

7. Write an explicit rule for the total number of pieces of fencing needed for any fence length using Wayne's table.

8. a) To build a fence, it is going to take 182 stages of the pattern. Use both Cassandra's and Wayne's explicit rules to determine the number of pieces of fencing needed. Do both rules give the same result? Why or why not?

   b) What stage of the fence uses 142 pieces of fencing? 370 pieces of fencing? Show your solution steps.

Equivalent Expressions Revisited

Cassandra and Wayne saw different patterns in the fence problem and wrote what looked like different explicit rules. Recall that equations describing the same pattern are equivalent. Equivalent equations or expressions can be simplified to the same equation or expression.

9. Show mathematically why Cassandra's and Wayne's explicit rules are equivalent by combining like terms.

10. Answer the following questions about Cassandra's and Wayne's rules: $T = 3n + 1$ and $T = (n + 1) + 2n$.

   a) What does the n in each equation represent? What does the T represent?

   b) Show how $3n$ is represented in the drawings. Show how $2n$ is represented in the drawings.

   c) What does the $n + 1$ represent in Wayne's rule?

   d) Does the $+ 1$ represent the same thing in both expressions: $3n + 1$ and $(n + 1) + 2n$? Explain.

   e) How is the recursive rule for the fence pattern related to the simplified explicit rule?

Here is a pattern that is sometimes used to build railings around decks. Notice how many pieces of wood are used for each stage.

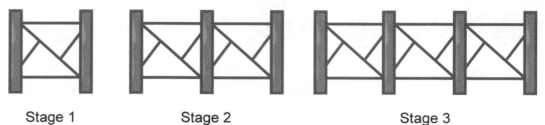

Stage 1   Stage 2   Stage 3

11. **a)** Make an expanded table for this railing pattern that compares the stage number and the total number of pieces of wood in each stage.

b) Explain in words any patterns you noticed in how the railing for each stage was constructed.

c) Find a recursive rule and an explicit rule.

d) How is your explicit rule represented in the table and in the drawing of the deck railing? Explain how the symbols in your rule are related to the drawing and the table values.

e) Write an equivalent explicit rule. Show that your rules are equivalent.

Is it possible to have different explicit rules for the same pattern? Why or why not? Use examples from this lesson.

Write About It

1. Why is it useful to write explicit rules for patterns instead of recursive rules? How is it possible for two students to find different explicit rules for the same pattern? Use an example and pictures to explain.

2. Mr. Whitmore, a middle school teacher, asked his students to build some patterns using blocks. Below are the first three stages of a "growing giant" pattern created by one of his students, Jake. At each subsequent stage, Jake adds an extra triangle to each arm and each leg.

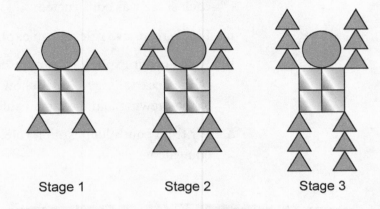

Stage 1   Stage 2   Stage 3

   a) Describe the pattern in words. Indicate what stays the same and what varies between each stage.

   b) Describe what Stage 42 would look like.

   c) Make an expanded table with three columns for this pattern. In the first column list the stage number. List the total number of blocks needed for each figure in the second column. In the third column, record patterns you observed in the total number of blocks such as what is constant and what changes each time. Fill in your table for Stages 4, 5 and 6.

   d) How many blocks will it take to build Stage 42?

   e) Write an explicit rule for this pattern.

   f) If it took 73 blocks to make a giant, what stage is that? How many of the blocks would be triangles?

3. Two students are trying to find equivalent expressions for $2(3 + 2x)$. Tara thinks that $2(5x)$ is equivalent, and Will thinks that $6 + 2x$ is equivalent. Are their expressions equivalent to $2(3 + 2x)$? Explain your reasoning.

Use the pattern below to answer Questions 4, 5, and 6. The pattern is built by adding two squares (one on the top and one on the bottom) to the previous figure.

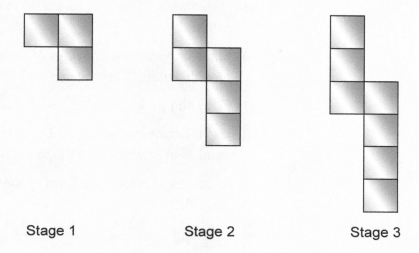

Stage 1   Stage 2   Stage 3

4. **a)** Draw Stages 1–5. Shade the drawings to indicate patterns. What is the same in each figure and what has changed?

   b) Make an expanded table. Record any patterns you notice in the number of squares.

   c) Write an explicit rule for the number of squares in each stage.

   d) Explain how the numbers and variable in your explicit rule are represented in the drawings of the pattern.

5. Write a different explicit rule for the number of squares in each stage of Question 4. Show that the two rules are equivalent.

6. Examine again the square pattern above. This time, consider the perimeter of each figure.

   a) Make a table that shows the perimeter of the first five stages of the pattern. The side length of each small square is 1 unit.

   b) Describe any numerical patterns you notice in the table.

   c) Write an explicit rule.

   d) What connections are there between the numbers in the explicit rule and the numerical patterns in the table?

7. Examine the table of a linear pattern.

Stage Number	1	2	3	4	5	6	10	27		
Number of Toothpicks	6	11	16	21					36	91

a) Describe any patterns you notice in the first four stages of the pattern.

b) Make up your own drawings of toothpick structures that follow this growth pattern. Show Stages 1–3.

c) Copy and fill in the rest of the table.

d) Use the patterns you noticed to work backwards and determine the number of toothpicks in Stage 0.

8. Use blocks or toothpicks to create geometric patterns for the following explicit rules.

a) $T = 3n$

b) $T = 2n + 2$

c) $T = 4n + 1$

Think Beyond

9. Examine the pattern below.

a) Draw Stages 4 and 5.

  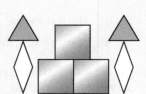 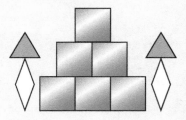

Stage 1   Stage 2   Stage 3

b) Describe the pattern in words and with a recursive rule.

c) Find an explicit rule for the total number of blocks in each stage.

d) Use your rule to find the total number of blocks in Stage 80.

e) Is this a linear pattern? Why or why not?

10. Make a chart of x- and y-values for the equation $y = |x|$ when $x = -7, -4, -1, 0, 2, 6$ and 8. Graph these points on the coordinate plane. Describe the shape of the graph.

11. A square has side lengths of $13\frac{1}{9}$ centimeters.

    a) List formulas that can be used to find the area and the perimeter of the square.

    b) Calculate the area and the perimeter of the square.

12. William was asked to place these rational numbers in order from least to greatest: $-\frac{11}{12}, -\frac{11}{15}, -\frac{11}{13}$.

    He said $-\frac{11}{12} < -\frac{11}{13} < -\frac{11}{15}$. Is he right or wrong? Explain.

13. Find the measure of each angle.

    a)

    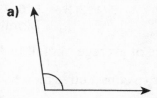

    b)

14. Solve for f: $\frac{f}{7} - 1 = -13$.

    A. 90

    B. -90

    C. -91

    D. -84

Linking Graphs, Tables and Equations

→ Start It Off

Average Rainfall in Atlanta, GA

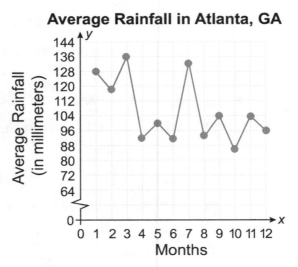

1. What is the range of average rainfall in Atlanta, Georgia?

2. Between which two consecutive months is the difference in average rainfall the greatest?

3. What does the coordinate (9, 104) represent?

4. Based on this graph, what is the mean of the average monthly rainfall amounts in Atlanta, Georgia?

Many high school, college and professional teams have mascots—funny figures that help people identify with a particular sports team. Mascots perform for the crowds and encourage the fans to cheer at important points in a game. Many mascots, like Otto the Orange (Syracuse University) and Mr. Met (New York Mets), are quite unique. Other mascot characters, such as eagles, tigers and bulldogs, are used by many teams.

The Whittenville School teams have a blue jay as a mascot. The team jerseys all have a geometric design built from seven tangram puzzle pieces. When players run out to the field and stand next to each other, it looks like a growing flock of birds!

Stage 1

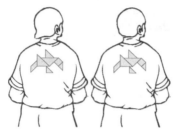

Stage 2

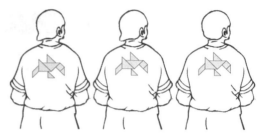

Stage 3

Imagine this pattern continuing with one more player joining the current players for each subsequent stage.

1. **a)** Make a table of data that records the stage number and the total number of puzzle pieces displayed on the jerseys of the players at that stage. Complete the table for Stages 1–8.

    b) Determine the recursive rule that relates each number of puzzle pieces to the next.

    c) Create a graph that relates the number of players to the total number of puzzle pieces displayed on their jerseys. Put the number of players on the horizontal axis and label your axes.

2. Should the points on the graph be connected? Why or why not?

From the graph, the relationship looks linear. But is it? When a relationship between two variables is linear, specific patterns occur in the graph, in the recursive rule, and in the table of corresponding data.

- A linear relationship between two variables produces a straight-line graph. Your graph of the number of puzzle pieces for different stages should look like a straight line.

- If the recursive rule describing the change from a previous term to the next involves adding the same positive or negative amount, then the relationship is linear. The sequence of our data on the number of puzzle pieces on the jerseys is described by *new = previous + 7*.

- From the table we can see that one variable is changing in a consistent way in relationship with the other. In a linear relationship, as the input value changes by 1 unit, the output quantity changes by a constant value. Our data show that as the stage number increases by 1, the number of puzzle pieces increases by 7.

3. a) Give the explicit rule or equation for this pattern. Let *n* represent the number of players and *P* represent the total number of puzzle pieces on their jerseys.

   b) How are the recursive rule and the explicit rule for this linear situation related?

Here is a table of data for another linear relationship.

Input (*x*)	Output (*y*)
0	0
1	−4
2	−8
3	−12
4	−16
5	−20
6	−24
7	−28

4. a) Determine the recursive rule for this linear relationship.

   b) Determine the explicit rule for this linear relationship.

   c) How are the recursive rule and the explicit rule for this linear situation related?

Example

Recall the giant pattern from Lesson 3.3 On Your Own. In each subsequent stage, a triangle is added to both arms and both legs.

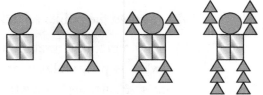

Stage 0   Stage 1   Stage 2   Stage 3

Stage Number (*n*)	Total Number of Blocks
0	5
1	9
2	13
3	17
4	21
5	25
n	$4n + 5$

Giant Patterns

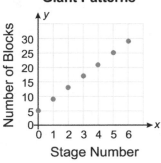

Example continued

Linear relationships between two variables can be shown using drawings, tables, graphs and equations.

Drawing: The description along with the pictures show that every giant was built using 5 fixed blocks. Subsequent stages increase by the same amount each time, 4 blocks, which are used to build his arms and legs.

Table: For each increase by 1 in the stage number, the total number of blocks increases by 4.

Graph: The coordinate points are in a straight line. The graph starts at $(0, 5)$. Each subsequent point is 4 units up and 1 unit over.

Equations: The recursive rule is *new = previous* + 4. The explicit rule is $T = 4n + 5$, where T represents the total number of blocks and n represents the stage number.

5. **a)** How are the recursive rule and the explicit rule for this linear relationship related?

   b) How is the changing part of this pattern shown in the drawing? In the table? In the graph? In the explicit rule, $T = 4n + 5$?

   c) How is the constant or fixed part of this pattern shown in the drawing? In the table? In the graph? In the explicit rule, $T = 4n + 5$?

Explore whether the following geometric patterns represent linear relationships. For each pattern, answer Questions 6–9.

Pattern A

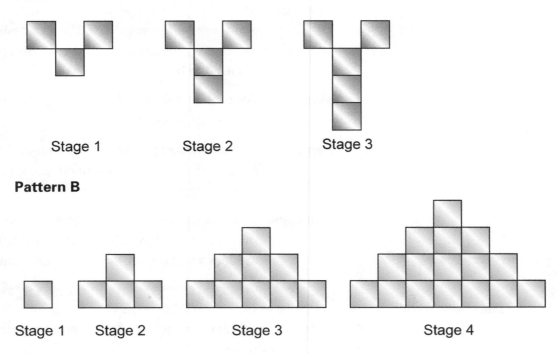

Stage 1   Stage 2   Stage 3

Pattern B

Stage 1   Stage 2   Stage 3   Stage 4

6. Make a table for the first seven stages that compares the stage number with the total number of squares in each stage.

7. Write an equation for the explicit rule. Define your variables.

8. **a)** Graph the equation. Make sure to label the axes and give the graph a title.

   b) Should the points on this graph be connected? Why or why not?

9. Explain using patterns from the table, the graph and the explicit rule whether the relationship is linear or not.

**rap It Up**

What are the characteristics of a linear relationship? How are the characteristics of linear relationships displayed in drawings, tables, graph and recursive rules?

LESSON 3.4

SECTION 3

On Your Own

Write About It

1. Make up a geometric pattern where there is a linear relationship between two variables. Explain why it is linear using tables, graphs, pictures and rules. Draw another example of a geometric pattern that is not linear.

2. Examine the geometric pattern of toothpicks below.

Stage 1   Stage 2   Stage 3

a) Build a table of values comparing the stage number and the total number of toothpicks. Identify the recursive rule. Describe it using the terms *new* and *previous*.

b) Write the explicit rule as an equation. Define your variables.

c) Sketch a graph of the first six ordered pairs (stage number, number of toothpicks).

d) Is the relationship between the variables linear or not? Explain.

3. a) Kelly works in a fast-food restaurant after school. She makes $7.50 an hour. Copy and complete the table to show what Kelly would be paid for different numbers of hours worked.

Hours, h	1	2	3	4	5	8	15	20
Pay (dollars), p								

b) Write an equation that shows how much money Kelly earns working after school. Define your variables.

c) Is the relationship between hours worked and pay linear? How do you know?

4. Patrick babysits his cousins after school. He makes $10 per hour. Write an equation that can be used to determine how much money Patrick earns babysitting.

5. a) Graph the equation in Question 4.

b) Describe what a table of values that compares hours worked and pay for Patrick's babysitting job would look like.

c) Should the points on this graph be connected? Why or why not?

6. Examine the graph below of the weight of baby Joel.

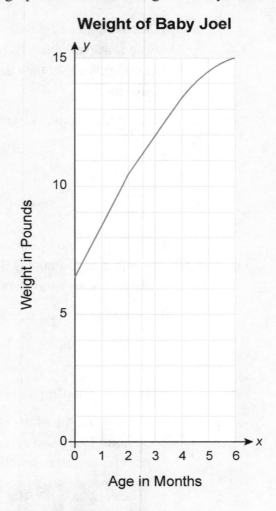

Weight of Baby Joel

a) Is the relationship between age and weight linear? Explain.

b) Build a table of approximate values for this relationship. Show how the table of values supports your answer to Part a.

c) Based on this graph, when did Joel gain the most weight? How can you tell?

7. You can decide if a relationship between two variables is linear by looking at a graph or at a table of values. Which do you prefer and why?

8. David and Jeff were talking about straight-line graphs. Jeff wasn't sure the following was considered a straight line. Is a slanted line a "straight line"? Is the relationship between the number of tablespoons and teaspoons linear? Explain.

Tablespoon and Teaspoon Equivalencies

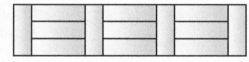

Many patterns used for walkways are made from pieces of bluestone. Examine the bluestone walkway pattern below. Use it to answer Questions 9–11.

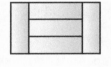 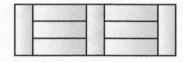

Stage 1   Stage 2   Stage 3

9. **a)** Find an explicit rule that lets you determine the total number of pieces of bluestone needed to make any stage. Use a table.

Hint
See page 158

b) How many pieces of bluestone are needed for a walkway that takes 25 stages to complete?

c) If each piece of bluestone is 3 feet long and 1 foot wide, how long is the 25-stage walkway?

10. Find an equivalent rule for the bluestone walkway pattern that lets you determine the total number of pieces of bluestone needed for any stage. Explain why your two rules are equivalent.

Hint
See page 158

11. a) Peter said that he thinks a rule that works for the bluestone pattern is $4(n + 1)$. Do you agree or disagree? Explain your reasoning.

b) Maria suggested that a rule for the bluestone pattern is $3n + (n + 1)$. Is this expression equivalent to $4n + 1$? Why or why not?

12. Different shapes can be put together to make "chains." For example, square and regular pentagon chains are shown below.

| Stage 1 | Stage 2 | Stage 3 | Stage 4 |

Square Chains

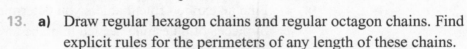

Regular Pentagon Chains

a) Create tables for each pattern that compare the stage number and the perimeter of the chain at that stage. Assume the side length of each square and pentagon is 1 unit.

b) Write explicit rules for each pattern so you can find the perimeter of a chain at any stage.

c) Describe what a graph of the square chain pattern perimeters would look like. Use words such as *increasing, decreasing, linear, nonlinear* and *steepness*.

Think Beyond

13. a) Draw regular hexagon chains and regular octagon chains. Find explicit rules for the perimeters of any length of these chains.

b) Why is it important that the figures in each chain are regular polygons?

c) Write a rule that can be used to determine the perimeter of any regular polygon chain of any length. Define your variables.

14. Write an equation that indicates that the sum of the interior angles in this pentagon is 540°. Find the value of *x*.

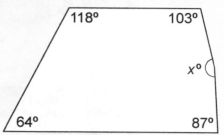

15. Write these percents as decimals and fractions in simplest form.

    a) 104%

    b) 84%

    c) 3%

    d) 20%

    e) 36%

16. You buy a T-shirt that costs $18.80. At the register, you find out the T-shirt is 15% off. What is the new price?

    A. $2.82

    B. $15.98

    C. $21.62

    D. $18.65

17. Trent had to decide if this statement was true or false. Comment on his answer.

    (True) or False
    Equilateral triangles are the only type of triangles that have congruent sides.

18. Who is traveling at a faster speed—Juanita, who covers 250 miles in 6 hours in a car, or Luis, who travels 360 miles in $8\frac{1}{2}$ hours on a bus? What is the unit rate for each person's vehicle?

Optional Technology Lesson for this section available in your eBook

Sum It Up

Linear Relationships

One type of mathematical relationship between two variables is a linear relationship.

- Linear relationships can be represented in staged pattern drawings that show a constant increase or decrease at each stage. This particular pattern continues by adding two additional squares to each subsequent stage.

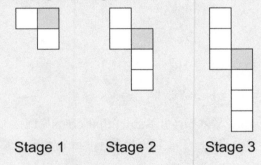

Stage 1   Stage 2   Stage 3

- Linear relationships can be represented in data tables. In the pattern above, as the stage number increases by 1, the number of squares increases by 2.

Stage Number	Total Number of Squares	Constant + Variation
1	3	1 + 2
2	5	1 + 4
3	7	1 + 6
4	9	1 + 8
n	$1 + 2n$	$1 + 2n$

- The recursive rule for the geometric pattern above is *new = previous* + 2. If the recursive rule adds the same amount from one value to the next value, then the relationship is linear.

- Explicit rules describe the relationship between the two variables. Explicit rules enable you to find the output value (in this case, total number of squares) for any input value (stage number). The explicit rule for this pattern is $T = 2n + 1$ where n is the stage number and T is the total number of squares.

■ The graph of a linear relationship is a continuous line or a set of points located on a line. The following graphs show linear relationships.

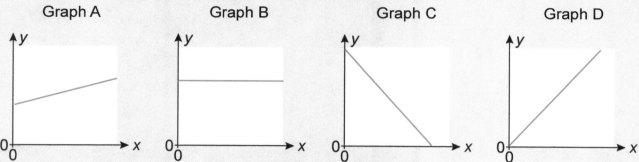

Graph A   Graph B   Graph C   Graph D

■ Some linear relationships are increasing. In these cases, as the input, or x-values, increase the output, or y-values, also increase. Graphs A and D show increasing linear relationships.

■ Some linear relationships are decreasing. In a decreasing relationship, as the input values increase, the output values decrease. Graph C is an example of a decreasing linear relationship.

■ Some linear relationships are neither increasing nor decreasing, such as Graph B. In Graph B, the output values are the same for all inputs.

Nonlinear Relationships

Not all relationships between variables are linear. One nonlinear relationship is shown below with an equation, table, graph and geometric pattern.

Equation: $S = n^2$

Table:

Stage number	Number of Squares (S)
1	1
2	4
3	9
4	16
5	25
n	n^2

Graph:

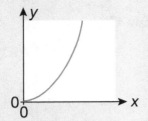

Drawing:

Stage 1   Stage 2   Stage 3

MATHEMATICALLY SPEAKING

Do you know what these mathematical terms mean?

▶ average speed   ▶ linear relationship   ▶ rate

▶ decreasing linear relationship   ▶ nonlinear relationship   ▶ speed

▶ increasing linear relationship

SECTION 3

Study Guide

Representing Linear Patterns Using
Equations, Graphs and Tables

MATERIALS LIST

▶ Centimeter grid
paper

Part 1. What did you learn?

1. Lucas runs a snack booth at the Indianapolis 500. He made the following observations about race day:

   (1) Every hour, the total number of hot dogs sold increases by 35.

   (2) As the race day goes on, five fewer customers order food each hour.

   (3) Each cook earns $30 per hour.

   (4) The number of people who order ice cream changes each hour, depending on the time of day.

   a. In each situation, identify the two variables being described.

   b. Determine whether the relationship described in each observation is increasing linear, decreasing linear, or nonlinear.

2. Donnie decided that he was watching too many sports shows. He began to decrease the time he spent watching sports by the same number of minutes each week. He kept a graph of the number of minutes of sports he watched each week for the first 11 weeks of his plan.

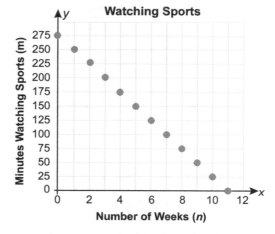

   a. Is the relationship between the week number and the number of minutes Donnie watches sports increasing linear, decreasing linear, or nonlinear? How do you know?

   b. Write a recursive rule for the relationship between the number of weeks and the number of minutes Donnie watches sports.

3. Good and Healthy Granola is sold by the pound. Each pound costs $4.80.

   a. Create a table to show the cost per quarter-pound of 0, 1, and 2 pounds of granola.

   b. Write an explicit rule that could be used to find the total cost, c, of buying n pounds of Good and Healthy Granola.

4. DeWayne created a pattern using pattern blocks.

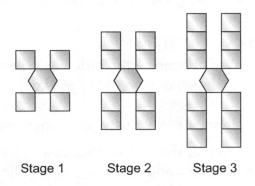

   Stage 1   Stage 2   Stage 3

   a. Copy and complete the chart below.

Stage Number	Total Number of Blocks	Number of Hexagons + Number of Squares
1		
2		
3		
4		
5		
6		
7		
8		
n		

   b. Write a recursive rule for DeWayne's pattern.

   c. Write an explicit rule for DeWayne's pattern.

   d. Is the relationship between stage number and total number of blocks linear? Why or why not?

   e. How many pattern blocks are needed for Stage 43?

5. Fiona created the pattern below using square tiles.

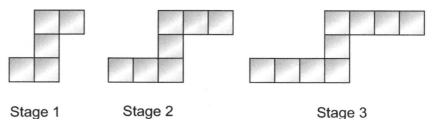

Stage 1   Stage 2   Stage 3

a. Copy and shade in the pictures of Stages 1–3 to show what is the constant and what is the varying quantity.

b. Copy and complete the chart below. Use your shading from Part a to complete the third column.

Stage Number	Total Number of Blocks	Constant + Variation
1		
2		
3		
4		
5		
6		
7		
8		
n		

c. Write a recursive rule for Fiona's pattern.

d. Write an explicit rule for Fiona's pattern.

e. Graph the explicit rule you wrote. Label the axes and give the graph a title.

f. Should the points on this graph be connected? Why or why not?

g. How many pattern blocks are needed for Stage 51?

6. Use the pattern from Question 5 again. Draw Stages 1–4.

    a. Identify a different growth pattern than the one you used for Question 5. Shade on the pictures a different constant and a different varying quantity.

    b. Copy and complete the following chart. Use your shading from part a to complete the third column.

Stage Number	Total Number of Blocks	Constant + Variation
1		
2		
3		
4		
5		
6		
7		
8		
n		

    c. Use your pattern to find a recursive rule for the pattern.

    d. Use your pattern to find an explicit rule for the pattern.

    e. Is your answer from Part c of Question 5 the same as your answer from Part c in Question 6? Why or why not?

    f. Is the explicit rule from Question 5 equivalent to your explicit rule from Question 6? Explain.

7. Match each table with one graph, one recursive rule, and one explicit rule.

Table	Graph	Recursive Rule	Explicit Rule
a. <table><tr><th>x</th><th>y</th></tr><tr><td>−2</td><td>−6</td></tr><tr><td>−1</td><td>−3</td></tr><tr><td>0</td><td>0</td></tr><tr><td>1</td><td>3</td></tr><tr><td>2</td><td>6</td></tr></table>	**e.**	**i.** Add −3 each time.	**m.** $y = 2x + 3$
b. <table><tr><th>x</th><th>y</th></tr><tr><td>−2</td><td>2</td></tr><tr><td>−1</td><td>1</td></tr><tr><td>0</td><td>0</td></tr><tr><td>1</td><td>−1</td></tr><tr><td>2</td><td>−2</td></tr></table>	**f.**	**j.** Add 2 each time.	**n.** $y = 3x$
c. <table><tr><th>x</th><th>y</th></tr><tr><td>−2</td><td>−1</td></tr><tr><td>−1</td><td>1</td></tr><tr><td>0</td><td>3</td></tr><tr><td>1</td><td>5</td></tr><tr><td>2</td><td>7</td></tr></table>	**g.**	**k.** Add −1 each time.	**o.** $y = −3x + 4$

Table	Graph	Recursive Rule	Explicit Rule
d. 	x	y		**l.** Add 3 each time.	**p.** $y = {}^-x$
	-2	10			

d.

x	y
-2	10
-1	7
0	4
1	1
2	-2

h.

l.
Add 3 each time.

p.
$y = {}^-x$

Part 2. What went wrong?

8. Dina was asked the following multiple-choice question on a recent quiz.

> Yuri eats energy bars to prepare for athletic competitions. One day, Yuri bought two of his favorite kind of energy bar for a total of $5. Another day, he bought three of the same kind of energy bar for $7.50. Which of the following could be used to find c, the cost of any number, n, of energy bars?
>
> **A.** $2.50n = c$ **C.** $2.50 + c = n$
>
> **B.** $2.50 + n = c$ **D.** $2.50c = n$

Dina chose letter D and it was marked wrong. Why is D the wrong choice? Which is the correct choice?

Unit Study Guide

Part 1. What did you learn?

SECTION 1

1. Explain the distributive property of multiplication over addition to a friend. How does this property work? Give several examples showing this property in use.

2. Colleen wrote expressions to find the areas of three rectangles. Here is her work:

   Rectangle A: 3(30) + 3(0.5)
   Rectangle B: 12(20) + 12(4)
   Rectangle C: 16(30) − 16(2)

   Use Colleen's expressions to complete the following:

   a. Sketch and label each rectangle.

   b. Write the dimensions of each rectangle.

   c. Use Colleen's expressions to determine the area of each rectangle.

3. Colleen drew her own rectangle with an area of 96 square units. It is pictured below.

   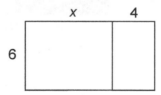

   a. Use the distributive property to represent the area of the rectangle.

   b. Expand the expression.

   c. Find x.

4. Determine if the variables in each of the following situations represent: (i) related varying quantities, (ii) many values, (iii) a specific value, or (iv) a set of numbers.

 a. The volume of a sphere can be calculated using the formula $V = \left(\frac{4}{3}\right)\pi r^3$ where V stands for the volume of the sphere and r stands for the radius of the sphere.

 b. Joanie earned $8 per hour raking her neighbor's lawn. Joanie earned a total of $60. The equation $8x = 60$ can be used to determine the total number of hours Joanie raked.

 c. Sam practices playing the trombone between 20 and 40 minutes each night. Let m represent the number of minutes Sam practices.

 d. Didi computed $43.5 + 17 + 6.5$ using the equivalent expression $43.5 + 6.5 + 17$ because she knows that $a + b + c = a + c + b$ (where a, b and c are real numbers).

5. Graph the values that make $x + 3 < {}^-3$ true when x is a real number.

6. Graph the values that make $4 - c > 12$ true when c is an integer.

7. Match each expression in Column A with the correct equivalent expression in Column B.

Column A	Column B
a. $8m + 5d + 12 - d$	**e.** $8m + 16$
b. $8m + 8 + 4m + 4$	**f.** $32md + 12$
c. $4 + 8m + 12$	**g.** $8m + 4d + 12$
d. $(8m)(4d) + (12)$	**h.** $12m + 12$

8. Fill in the blanks in the following sentences:

   a. The multiplicative inverse of 4 is _____.

   b. The multiplicative inverse of $1\frac{3}{8}$ is _____.

   c. The additive inverse of 0 is _____.

   d. The additive inverse of -22.5 is _____.

   e. The _____ of a pair of additive inverses is zero.

   f. The product of a pair of multiplicative inverses is _____.

9. Illustrate each of the following properties with an example using variables and with an example using numbers.

	Property	Example using Variables	Example using Numbers
a.	associative property of addition		
b.	associative property of multiplication		
c.	commutative property of addition		
d.	commutative property of multiplication		
e.	distributive property of multiplication over addition		
f.	identity property of addition		
g.	identity property of multiplication		

10. Determine whether each statement is true or false.

   a. The additive inverse of zero is zero.

   b. The multiplicative inverse of zero is zero.

   c. In a pair of non-zero additive inverses, one number is always between 0 and 1.

   d. In a pair of non-zero multiplicative inverses, one number is always between -1 and 1.

   e. For any number n, the multiplicative inverse is always of the form $\frac{1}{n}$.

11. Find the missing term in each of the equations below.

    a. $9a + 8 - \underline{\hspace{2cm}} - 3 = a + 5$

    b. $3a + 2b + 7b + \underline{\hspace{2cm}} = 9b$

    c. $\underline{\hspace{2cm}} c \cdot \frac{1}{9} = 5c$

    d. $\left(\frac{9}{4}\right)\left(\frac{4}{9}\right)(\underline{\hspace{2cm}})a = 12a$

12. In the formula $\frac{180(n-2)}{n} = a$, n represents the number of sides of a regular polygon and a represents the measure of each interior angle. Use the formula to find the measure of an interior angle (in degrees) of each of the following polygons:

    a. equilateral triangle

    b. regular hexagon

    c. regular 12-sided polygon (dodecagon)

SECTION 2

13. Tim is right-handed, but he is trying to learn how to shoot baskets with his left hand. Tim decided to count the number of left-handed shots he made during his practice sessions. On Tuesday morning, he made three times as many baskets as he did on Monday. He stopped for a break. In the afternoon, he made five more baskets for a total of 41 baskets.

    a. Use a flowchart to determine the number of baskets Tim made on Monday.

    b. Write an equation that could be used to determine the number of baskets Tim made on Monday.

    c. Write the steps to solve your equation from Part b.

14. Use inverse operations to find the value of x in the flowchart below.

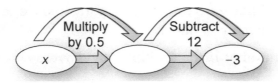

15. Solve each equation. Show your work.

    a. $-4x = 22$

    b. $6(c + 2) = 72$

    c. $9 - 3n = 8$

    d. $3\frac{1}{4}m = 39$

    e. $\frac{5}{6}w + 2 = 12$

16. Compare and contrast solving equations using the balancing method and solving equations using inverse operations (or undoing). In Question 15, how did you decide which method to use for each equation?

17. Match each pair of equations in Column A with the property in Column B that is used to solve the equation. Then, find the solution to the equation in Column C.

Column A	Column B	Column C
(a) $\frac{2}{3}n = -8$ $\frac{3}{2} \cdot \frac{2}{3}n = -8 \cdot \frac{3}{2}$	(f) commutative property of multiplication	(k) $n = 2$
(b) $n - 12.5 = 28.75$ $n + {}^-12.5 + 12.5 = 28.75 + 12.5$	(g) multiplication property of equality	(l) $n = -12$
(c) $1\frac{2}{3} + n + 3\frac{1}{3} = 7$ $n + 5 = 7$	(h) associative property of addition	(m) $n = 12$
(d) $\frac{3}{4} \cdot n \cdot 1\frac{1}{3} = 12$ $\frac{3}{4} \cdot \frac{4}{3} \cdot n = 12$	(i) addition property of equality	(n) $n = -2$
(e) $(3.75 + n) + 6.25 = 8$ $10 + n = 8$	(j) commutative property of addition	(o) $n = 41.25$

18. Nat and Morton solved the same equation using two different methods. Nat said, "I added −3 to both sides. Then, divided both sides by 5." Morton said, "I subtracted 3 from both sides. Then, I multiplied both sides by $\frac{1}{5}$." Can both methods solve the same equation correctly? Why or why not?

SECTION 3

19. Remember Elizabeth, the reluctant runner from Lesson 1 in Section 3? After successfully completing the Flying Pig Marathon, she decided to enter the New York City marathon. In this race, Elizabeth ran 2 miles every quarter-hour.

   a. Create a table showing the total distance Elizabeth ran during the first 2 hours of the race. Use quarter-hour intervals for time.

   b. Look back at the graph you made for Elizabeth's progress during the Flying Pig Marathon. If you were to make a graph of her progress in the New York City marathon, how would this graph compare to the Flying Pig Marathon graph? Explain.

   c. Write an explicit rule that could be used to find Elizabeth's distance, *d*, after any number of hours, *h*.

20. Elizabeth ran the New York City Marathon with her friend Cleo. Cleo made this graph of her progress during the first 2 hours of the race.

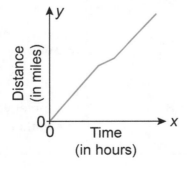

Is the relationship between Cleo's time and the distance she ran linear? Why or why not?

21. Ralphie is a huge fan of NASCAR. He is saving up money to travel to the Indy 500. He saves $25 each week by walking dogs after school and saving his weekly allowance. He made the graph below but forgot to label the axes.

Savings plan

a. What do you think is the label for the x-axis of Ralphie's graph? The y-axis?

b. What do you think the points (0, 0) and (10, 250) tell us about Ralphie's savings?

c. Create a table for the data points in the graph.

d. Write an explicit rule for the relationship between the variables in your table. Be sure to define your variables.

22. Hannah created the "H" pattern pictured below.

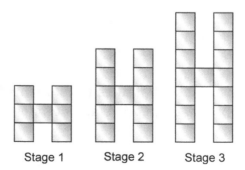

Stage 1   Stage 2   Stage 3

a. Copy and complete the table below.

Stage Number	Total Number of Squares	Constant + Variation
1		
2		
3		
4		
5		
6		
7		
8		
n		

b. Write a recursive rule for Hannah's pattern.

c. Write an explicit rule for Hannah's pattern.

d. What is the relationship between the recursive rule and the explicit rule?

e. Is the relationship between stage number and total number of blocks linear? How do you know?

f. How many pattern blocks are needed for stage 71?

23. Nalesh and his classmates investigated the following pentagon chain pattern.

Regular Pentagon Chains

   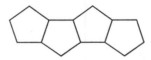

When his teacher asked what rules the students found to calculate p, the perimeter of any stage number, n, he heard the following:

a. $5n - 2n + 2 = P$

b. $3n + 2 = P$

c. $5n - 2(n - 1) = P$

d. $4n - n - 2 = P$

Which of these rules are correct? How do you know?

24. Larry's teacher used the expression $4d$ to represent the number of quarters in d dollars. Larry is confused by this because he learned in fifth grade that $4d$ meant four dollars since "we always had to label our numbers." What do you think $4d$ means?

25. Jonah wrote $n + 4 = t$ (where n stands for the stage number and t stands for the total number of squares) for the explicit rule for the "H" pattern in Question 22. His teacher told him this rule would not work. The teacher said, "I think you are confused about the difference between recursive and explicit rules." What is wrong with Jonah's explicit rule? How could you help him find and fix his error?

26. Hoai's teacher asked her how to solve $18x = 9$. Hoai said, "We should undo multiplying by 18 by dividing by 18. This tells us that $x = 2$ since $18 \div 9 = 2$." Hoai's teacher said she was wrong. Why? What is Hoai's error? How can you help her fix it?

27. Heather tried to solve the equation $3 - 2m = 15$. Here is what Heather did:

$$3 - 2m = 15$$
$$3 - 2m + (-3) = 15 + (-3)$$
$$2m = 12$$
$$m = 6$$

What error(s) did Heather make? How can you help her find and fix her errors?

28. After learning about additive inverses and multiplicative inverses, Dom became very confused. He asked his teacher, "If we undo addition by adding the opposite, why don't we undo multiplication by multiplying by the opposite?" He even gave an example:

$$13 + n = 29$$
$$13 + n + {}^-13 = 29 + {}^-13$$
$$n = 16$$

If the above equation is true, then the equation below should also be true:

$$\frac{1}{3}n = 25$$
$$\frac{3}{1} \cdot \frac{1}{3}n = 25 \cdot \frac{3}{1}$$
$$n = {}^-75$$

What would you say or do to help Dom realize the error in his reasoning?

Glossary

addition property of equality The property that states that if the same number is added to both sides of an equation, the resulting expressions on each side remain equal.

Example:
For all real numbers a, b, and c, if $a = b$ then
$$a + c = b + c.$$
$$x + 4 = 19$$
$$x + 4 + {}^-4 = 19 + {}^-4 \quad \text{Add } {}^-4 \text{ to both sides.}$$
$$x + 0 = 15$$
$$x = 15$$

additive inverse The opposite of a number. The number that, when added to a given number, results in a sum of zero.

Example:
For all real numbers a, $a + (^-a) = 0$.
  ^-a is the additive inverse of a.
  a is the additive inverse of ^-a.

6 is the additive inverse of $^-6$.
$^-6$ is the additive inverse of 6.

algebra A branch of mathematics that generalizes and extends the ideas of arithmetic. Algebra uses symbols to represent numbers and express mathematical relationships.

associative property of addition The property that states that changing the grouping of addends does not change their sum.

Example:
For all real numbers a, b, and c:
  $a + (b + c) = (a + b) + c.$

$$3 + (7 + 4) = (3 + 7) + 4$$

associative property of multiplication The property that states that changing the grouping of factors does not change their product.

Example:
For all real numbers a, b, and c:
  $a \cdot (b \cdot c) = (a \cdot b) \cdot c.$

$$3 \cdot (6 \cdot 10) = (3 \cdot 6) \cdot 10$$

average speed The total distance an object traveled in a given time period divided by that time period.

Example:
A 100 mile trip driving at various speeds took 2 hours to complete. The average speed was $\frac{100}{2} = 50$ mph.

commutative property of addition The property that states that changing the order of the addends does not change their sum

Example:
For all real numbers a and b: $a + b = b + a.$

$$4 + 6 = 6 + 4$$

commutative property of multiplication The property that states that changing the order of factors does not change their product.

Example:
For all real numbers a and b: $a \cdot b = b \cdot a.$

$$5 \cdot 3 = 3 \cdot 5$$

constant A value that does not vary.

Example:

In the expression $x + 3$, 3 is a constant.

In the formula $A = \pi r^2$, π is a constant.

---

decreasing (linear) relationship A (linear) relationship in which an increase in the value of the input results in a decrease in the value of the output.

Example:

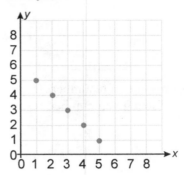

---

distributive property of multiplication over addition The property that states that to multiply a sum by a number, you can multiply each addend by the number and add the products.

Example:

For all real numbers a, b and c:

$a \cdot (b + c) = ab + ac$

$3 \cdot (5 + 8) = (3 \cdot 5) + (3 \cdot 8)$

---

distributive property of multiplication over subtraction The property that states that to multiply a difference by a number, you can multiply the minuend and the subtrahend by the number and find the difference of the products.

Example:

For all real numbers a, b and c:

$a \cdot (b - c) = a \cdot b - a \cdot c$

$7 \cdot (9 - 4) = (7 \cdot 9) - (7 \cdot 4)$

---

equation A mathematical sentence stating that two expressions are equal.

Example:

$\left(\frac{1}{a}\right)(a) = 1$

$3x + 4 = 7$

---

equivalent expressions Expressions that simplify to an equal value for all values of the variable(s) they contain.

Example:

$l + l + w + w$ and $2l + 2w$ are equivalent expressions for the perimeter of a rectangle.

---

evaluate (an expression) To substitute numerical values for a variable (or variables) in an expression, and then carry out the operations in the correct order resulting in a single numerical value.

Example: Evaluate: $3(x + y) - 2\,(10)$ for $x = 2$ and $y = 3$

$3(2 + 3) - 2\,(10) =$

$3(5) - 20 =$

$15 - 20 = -5$

---

expanded form (of an expression) The form of an expression composed of sums and/or differences of terms rather than the products of factors.

Example:

Factored form: $6(x + 2)$

Expanded form: $6x + 12$

---

explicit rule A rule that provides an output value directly from the application of the rule on an input value.

Example:

$t = 3n + 1$ is the explicit rule to determine the nth term of the sequence $\{4, 7, 10, 13, \ldots\}$.

For a circle of radius r, the area A is given by the explicit rule $A = \pi r^2$.

expression A mathematical phrase made of a combination of numbers, variables and/or operations.

Example:

$5x + 2$

πr^2

factored form (of an expression) The form of an expression composed of the product of factors rather than the sums and/or differences of terms.

Example:

Expanded form: $6x + 12$

Factored form: $6(x + 2)$

flowchart A graphic representation showing the sequence of the steps of an activity. In mathematics, it can represent the correct order of operations for simplifying or evaluating an expression or equation.

Example:

Evaluate $2 \cdot 3 + 5$.

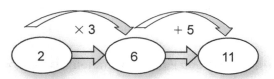

formula A rule or convention expressed using numbers, operations and variables.

Example:

To convert degrees Celsius (C) to degrees Fahrenheit (F), use the formula: $F = \frac{9}{5}C + 32$.

To find the circumference of a circle of radius r, use the formula: $C = 2\pi r$.

identity element A number that does not change other numbers when it operates on them.

Example:

additive identity is 0:

$a + 0 = a$
$5 + 0 = 5$

multiplicative identity is 1:

$a \cdot 1 = a$
$10 \cdot 1 = 10$

identity property of addition The property that states that any number added to the additive identity, 0, results in the original number.

Example:

For all real numbers a: $a + 0 = a$

$8 + 0 = 8$

identity property of multiplication The property that states that any number multiplied by the multiplicative identity, 1, results in the original number.

Example:

For all real numbers a: $a \cdot 1 = a$

$9 \cdot 1 = 9$

increasing (linear) relationship A (linear) relationship in which an increase in the value of the input results in an increase in the value of the output.

Example:

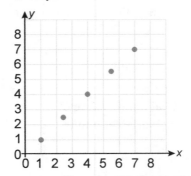

inequality A statement that uses the symbols > (greater than), < (less than), ≥ (greater than or equal to) and ≤ (less than or equal to) to indicate how one quantity relates to another in terms of being larger or smaller. The symbol ≠ also indicates an inequality but provides no further information on the relationship of the terms.

Example:

inverse operations Pairs of operations that undo each other.

Example:

Addition and Subtraction:
$$5 + 2 = 7 \qquad 7 - 2 = 5$$

Multiplication and Division:
$$5 \cdot 3 = 15 \qquad \frac{15}{3} = 5$$

Square and Square Root (for $n \geq 0$):
$$n \cdot n = n^2 \qquad \sqrt{n^2} = n$$

like terms Terms in an expression or equation that include the same variable(s), each raised to the same power(s); like terms can be combined to simplify expressions and equations.

Example:

In the expression $3 + 4x + 6 + 7x$, 3 and 6 are like terms, and $4x$ and $7x$ are like terms. Since $3 + 6 = 9$ and $4x + 7x = 11x$, we can simplify $3 + 4x + 6 + 7x$ as $9 + 11x$.

linear relationship A relationship between two variables whose ordered pairs form a straight line when graphed. The recursive rule for a linear relationship shows addition or subtraction of a constant at each step.

Example:

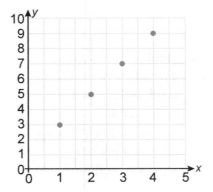

Recursive: *New = Previous + 2*

multiplication property of equality The property that states if the same number multiplies both sides of an equation, the resulting expressions on each side remain equal.

Example:

For all real numbers a, b and c, if $a = b$ then $a \cdot c = b \cdot c$.

$$3x = 27$$
$$\left(\tfrac{1}{3}\right)(3x) = \left(\tfrac{1}{3}\right)(27) \quad \text{Multiply both sides by } \left(\tfrac{1}{3}\right).$$
$$1x = 9$$
$$x = 9$$

---

multiplicative inverse A number that when multiplied by a given number results in a product of 1. The reciprocal of a number.

Example:

For all real numbers a where $a \neq 0$: $\left(\tfrac{1}{a}\right)(a) = 1$

$$\left(\tfrac{1}{7}\right)(7) = 1$$

$\tfrac{1}{7}$ is the multiplicative inverse of 7.

7 is the multiplicative inverse of $\tfrac{1}{7}$.

---

nonlinear relationship A relationship between two variables whose ordered pairs do not form a straight line.

Example:

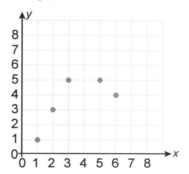

---

rate A comparison or relationship between two quantities that have different units of measure.

Example:

Speed: miles per hour

Density: pounds per square inch

Typing: words per minute

---

reciprocal One of two numbers whose product is 1. The multiplicative inverse of a number.

Example:

The reciprocal of 6 is $\tfrac{1}{6}$.

The reciprocal of $\tfrac{2}{3}$ is $\tfrac{3}{2}$.

---

recursive (iterative) rule A rule that is applied to the result of a previous application of itself; the input value is a previous output value of the rule.

Example:

Every day I save 25 cents of my lunch money and put it in a jar on my desk. Each day I can express the amount of money I have in the jar using the recursive rule: *new = previous + 25*.

solution A number or set of numbers that produces a true statement when substituted for a variable (or variables) in a mathematical sentence, such as an equation or inequality; the answer to a mathematical problem.

Example:

Equation: $5x = 10$ Solution: $x = 2$

Equation: $3x > 15$ Solution: $x > 5$

---

solve (an equation) The process of finding a solution to an equation.

Example:

Equation:

$$3x + 4 = 7$$

$$3x + 4 - 4 = 7 - 4$$

$$3x = 3$$

Solution: $x = 1$

---

speed The rate of motion or movement measured in a ratio of a distance measurement to a time measurement.

Example:

40 miles per hour

15 feet per second

---

term A number, a variable or a product of numbers and variables.

Example:

In the expression $3x^2 + x - 5$, the terms are $3x^2$, x, and 5.

---

variable A letter or other symbol used to represent a number or set of numbers in an expression or an equation.

Example:

$10x = 50$ The variable is x.

$5p + 3 > 20$ The variable is p.

$3\triangle = 7\square$ The variables are $\triangle$ and $\square$.

Hints

Lesson 1.1

On Your Own

Page 11, Question 9: $\mathbb{Z}$ represents the set of integers. The solution set when $x = \mathbb{Z}$ can only be an integer.

Page 12, Question 12a: How do you show that your mother is 24 years older than you?

Lesson 1.2

On Your Own

Page 18, Question 7: Divide each room into more familiar shapes and find the areas of the individual shapes.

Page 19, Question 9a: A YIELD sign has the shape of a triangle.

Page 19, Question 9b: The sum of the interior angles in a polygon is $S = 180 \cdot (n - 2)$ where n is the number of sides of the polygon and S is the sum.

Lesson 1.3

On Your Own

Page 28, Question 8: Use the glossary.

Page 28, Question 9: Use the identity property of multiplication.

Lesson 1.4

On Your Own

Page 38, Question 8: Consecutive numbers follow one another, such as 14 and 15. If you represent the first number using x, how can you represent the next number?

Page 39, Question 13: The commutative properties focus on the order of the terms and the associative properties focus on the grouping of the terms.

Lesson 2.1

On Your Own

Page 53, Question 6: Use a flowchart to represent the actions in the problem.

Page 54, Question 9: To start, divide by $\frac{1}{8}$.

Lesson 2.2

On Your Own

Page 62, Question 6a: Think about how to use 0 and 1 to produce equations with different values ($5 - 5 = 0$ and $5 \div 5 = 1$).

Lesson 2.3

On Your Own

Page 71, Question 3: The order of operations can be recalled using the mnemonic: PEMDAS.

Page 72, Question 6: First, rewrite subtraction equations as addition equations.

Page 72, Question 8: The variable represents many values if there are an infinite number of solutions. In other equations there is no value for the variable that makes the equation true.

Lesson 2.4

On Your Own

Page 80, Question 3: Draw a flowchart and fill in what you know to start.

Page 81, Question 10: $-k = (-1)k$

Lesson 3.1

On Your Own

Page 98, Question 3: Can you buy a fraction of a CD?

Page 99, Question 5a: Compare all the friends by examining how far they have each walked after the same number of seconds.

Lesson 3.2

On Your Own

Page 108, Question 3b: Look at the time increments and the distance increments in the table. Be sure to write your rule to take both into account.

Lesson 3.4

On Your Own

Page 129, Question 9a: Notice how one vertical piece to the left of three horizontal pieces are repeatedly drawn in each stage. There is always one extra vertical piece of bluestone to the right that is constant in every stage. Expand your table to include this information at each stage.

Page 129, Question 10: For this question, build a table of values. Notice how there are 5 pieces of bluestone in Stage 1: two vertical pieces and three horizontal pieces. Is this constant in all stages?

Index

S

simplifying   21, 26–28
  distributive property reverse of   35
  like terms   35
solution   3, 9, 156. (See also *equations, variable*).
solve (an equation)   3, 156
speed   96, 156
surface area   17
symbols   2–4, 27, 49. (See also *constant, variable.*)
  ϵ ("is an element of" or "is a member of")   4

T

temperature, formula for converting   18, 20
term(s)   35, 156
  like   35

U

undoing   56, 60, 62, 77, 78. (See also *inverse operations, working backwards.*)

V

values
  explicit rule and   56
variable(s)   3, 27, 156. (See also *constant, symbol.*)
  equations   4, 65, 83
  explicit rule and   104, 132
  formula and   15, 41
  generalized numbers   7
  graph   8, 93
  input/output   57, 104, 106
  linear relationships   91, 123, 127
  linking two   5
  meaning of   41
  nonlinear   133
  representing a specific value   3
  solving equations   3
  specific value for   4
  term   35
  varying quantities   4–6
varying quantities   4–6

W

working backwards   52, 120. (See also *inverse operations, undoing.*)